Kaplan Publishing are constantly finding new ways to make a difference to your studies and our exciting online resources really do offer something different to AAT students looking for exam success.

FOR THE FIRST TIME, KAPLAN'S AAT TEXTS COME WITH FREE EN-gage ONLINE RESOURCES SO THAT YOU CAN STUDY ANYTIME, ANYWHERE

Having purchased this Kaplan Text, you have access to the following online study materials:

- An online version of the Text
- Fixed Online Tests with instant answers

How to access your online resources

- **Kaplan Financial students** will already have a Kaplan EN-gage account and these extra resources will be available to you online. You do not need to register again, as this process was completed when you enrolled. If you are having problems accessing online materials, please ask your course administrator.
- **If you purchased through Kaplan Flexible Learning or via the Kaplan Publishing website** you will automatically receive an e-mail invitation to Kaplan EN-gage online. Please register your details using this e-mail to gain access to your content. If you do not receive the e-mail or book content, please contact Kaplan Flexible Learning.
- **If you are already a registered Kaplan EN-gage user** go to www.EN-gage.co.uk and log in. Select the 'add a book' feature and enter the ISBN number of this book and the unique pass key at the bottom of this card. Then click 'finished' or 'add another book'. You may add as many books as you have purchased from this screen.
- **If you are a new Kaplan EN-gage user** register at www.EN-gage.co.uk and click on the link contained in the e-mail we sent you to activate your account. Then select the 'add a book' feature, enter the ISBN number of this book and the unique pass key at the bottom of this card. Then click 'finished' or 'add another book'.

Your Code and Information

This code can only be used once for the registration of one book online. This registration will expire when the final sittings for the examinations covered by this book have taken place. Please allow one hour from the time you submitted your book details for us to process your request.

IPpa-mG2l-mAsl-00Lz

Please be aware that this code is case-sensitive and you will need to include the dashes within the passcode, but not when entering the ISBN. For further technical support, please visit www.EN-gage.co.uk

CASH MANAGEMENT

Qualifications and Credit Framework

Level 3 Diploma in Accounting

British Library Cataloguing-in-Publication Data

A catalogue record for this book is available from the British Library.

Published by
Kaplan Publishing UK
Unit 2, The Business Centre
Molly Millars Lane
Wokingham
Berkshire
RG41 2QZ

ISBN 978-0-85732-216-6

Printed in Great Britain by WM Print Ltd, Walsall.

We are grateful to the Association of Accounting Technicians for permission to reproduce past assessment materials and example tasks based on the new syllabus. The solutions to past answers and similar activities in the style of the new syllabus have been prepared by Kaplan Publishing.

CONTENTS

STUDY TEXT AND WORKBOOK

INTRODUCTION

HOW TO USE THESE MATERIALS

These Kaplan Publishing learning materials have been carefully designed to make your learning experience as easy as possible and to give you the best chance of success in your AAT assessments.

They contain a number of features to help you in the study process.

The sections on the Unit Guide, the Assessment and Study Skills should be read before you commence your studies.

They are designed to familiarise you with the nature and content of the assessment and to give you tips on how best to approach your studies.

STUDY TEXT

This study text has been specially prepared for the revised AAT qualification introduced in July 2010.

It is written in a practical and interactive style:

- key terms and concepts are clearly defined

- all topics are illustrated with practical examples with clearly worked solutions based on sample tasks provided by the AAT in the new examining style

- frequent practice activities throughout the chapters ensure that what you have learnt is regularly reinforced

- 'pitfalls' and 'examination tips' help you avoid commonly made mistakes and help you focus on what is required to perform well in your examination.

- clear advice as to which practice activities can be completed is given at the end of each chapter

WORKBOOK

The workbook comprises:

A question bank of practice activities with solutions, to reinforce the work covered in each chapter.

The questions are divided into their relevant chapters and students may either attempt these questions as they work through the textbook, or leave some or all of these until they have completed the textbook as a final revision of what they have studied

ICONS

The study chapters include the following icons throughout.

They are designed to assist you in your studies by identifying key definitions and the points at which you can test yourself on the knowledge gained.

 Definition

These sections explain important areas of Knowledge which must be understood and reproduced in an assessment

 Example

The illustrative examples can be used to help develop an understanding of topics before attempting the activity exercises

 Activity

These are exercises which give the opportunity to assess your understanding of all the assessment areas.

 Test your knowledge

At the end of each chapter these boxes will direct you to the Practice Activities that you can attempt after studying the chapter.

UNIT GUIDE

Cash management is divided into two units but for the purposes of assessment these units will be combined.

Principles of Cash Management (Knowledge)

3 credits

Cash Management (Skills)

3 credits

Purpose of the units

The AAT has stated that the general purpose of these units is to equip accounting technicians not only with an understanding of the theoretical principles of good cash management but also with the practical skills to undertake the preparation of cash budgets using a range of financial information, to select appropriate methods of financing cash shortfalls and to recommend suitable investment for surplus funds.

Learning objectives

In the Principles of Cash Management (knowledge) unit:

- Understand the principles of managing cash balances and deficits within an organisation

- Understand and be able to advise on options available for both raising finance and investing surplus cash

- Offer advice that should not be detrimental to the cash flow of normal business activities and should minimise risk to the organisation

In the Cash Management (skills) unit:

- Develop the skills necessary for managing cash balances to ensure the ongoing liquidity of an organisation

- Use forecasting techniques for predicting income and expenditure

- Prepare cash budgets that enable informed decision-making regarding both the borrowing and investing of surplus funds

Learning Outcomes and Assessment criteria

The unit consists of five learning outcomes, three for Knowledge and three for Skills, which are further broken down into Assessment criteria. These are set out in the following table with Learning Outcomes in bold type and Assessment criteria listed underneath each Learning Outcome. Reference is also made to the relevant chapter within the text.

Knowledge

To perform this unit effectively you will need to know and understand the following:

		Chapter
1	**Understand how the external environment impacts on how an organisation manages cash assets**	
1.1	Explain how government monetary policies affect an organisation's treasury functions	5
1.2	Explain how recording and accounting practices may vary in different parts of the organisation	2
1.3	Describe how an organisation's principles of cash management will be determined by their specific financial regulations, guidelines and security procedures	5
1.4	Identify statutory and other regulations relating to the management of cash balances in different types of organisations	4/5
2	**Be able to make informed decisions regarding the management of cash balances within an organisation**	
2.1	Identify the characteristics of the main types of cash receipts and payment of: regular revenue receipt; capital receipts; exceptional receipts and payments; drawings	2
2.2	Explain how an organisation can raise finance from a bank through overdrafts and loans, and the basic terms and conditions associated with each of these types of financing	4

		Chapter
2.3	Explain different types of investment, the risks and terms and conditions associated with them, including: certificates of deposit; government securities; local authority short term loans; shares	5
3	**Understand a range of accounting and other business techniques used to improve the efficiency of cash management procedures within an organisation.**	
3.1	Identify the component parts of cash budgets and how these are presented to aid decision making	2
3.2	Explain the effects of lagged receipts and payments upon an organisation's cash management	2
3.3	Describe the relationship between cash flow accounting and accounting for income and expenditure	1
3.4	Identify the principles of liquidity management	1
3.5	Explain techniques that can be used for estimating future trends: moving averages; allowance for inflation	3
3.6	Identify the ways to manage risk and exposure when investing, to minimise potential losses to the organisation	5

Skills

To perform this unit effectively you will need to be able to do the following.

		Chapter
1	**Prepare forecasts of income and expenditure for a given accounting period**	
1.1	Determine the likely pattern of cash flows over the accounting period, and anticipate any exceptional receipts or payments	2
1.2	Ensure forecasts of future cash payments and receipts agree with known income and expenditure trends	3
1.3	Prepare cash budgets and clearly indicate net cash requirements	2

2 Use forecasts to monitor cash flow within the organisation

2.1	Monitor cash receipts and payments against budget cash flow	3
2.2	Identify significant deviations from the cash budget and take corrective action within organisational policies	3

3 Use cash balances effectively

3.1	Observe the organisation's financial regulations and security procedures	4/5
3.2	Take account of trends in the economic and financial environment in managing cash balances	3
3.3	Manage cash, overdrafts and loans in order to maintain an adequate level of liquidity in lie with cash forecasts	4
3.4	Anticipate cash requirements and arrange overdraft and loan facilities on the most favourable terms available	4
3.5	Invest surplus finds according to organisational policy and within defined financial authorisation limits	5

Delivery guidance

The AAT have provided delivery guidance giving further details of the way in which the unit will be assessed.

The term cash in this Unit is used to include bank accounts as well as coins and notes and cash payments include cheque payments, BACS, direct debits and standing orders

The effective management of cash is not something that can be undertaken in isolation or without an awareness of the general financial environment in which organisations operate. Therefore it is important that learners have a basic awareness of how the banking sector is structured, the relationship between different financial institutions and understand that legal relationships exist between lenders and borrowers. Learners should also be introduced to the sort of financial terminology which they could encounter in the workplace such as fixed and floating charges, brokers, money markets. Though these areas are not specifically assessable they are essential background knowledge.

Assessment tasks may use some technical financial terminology however learners will only be expected to display knowledge or understanding of terms that are specifically noted in the delivery guidance and standards as assessable. The use of other terms will simply be to add reality to a task and the ability to undertake the task in a competent manner will not depend upon any detailed knowledge of such terminology.

Assessment tasks may relate to a range of different organisations including sole traders, partnerships and limited companies. Learners will not be expected to have any prior knowledge of the structure or accounting regulations of these organisations as they will simply be used as a background setting to enable assessment. Receipts and payments that might be organisation specific – for example, corporation tax – could be used in tasks but learners will simply be required to treat these cash flows in accordance with the instructions in the assessment data.

Liquidity

Adequate liquidity is often a key factor in contributing to the success or failure of trading organisations. Learners need to understand that cash is part of the working capital of the business and that the time taken to convert inventory, receivables and payables into cash affects the liquidity position of the organisation. Liquidity management involves monitoring cash flows through the working capital cycle, understanding that different types of cash flows have different timing patterns, using cash budgets to forecast and monitor the organisations liquidity position, arranging finance to cover expected cash shortfalls and investing cash surpluses to achieve maximum returns. A key principle of liquidity management is being able to recognise the indicators of possible future liquidity problems which include overtrading and overcapitalisation.

Through practical tasks, learners should be able to demonstrate they understand:

- The meaning of liquidity and be able to identify different forms of liquid assets How the circulation of working capital is demonstrated by the cash cycle

- Why liquidity/cash is important to a business both for daily operations and for its ability to meet future financial obligations

- The key principles of liquidity management

- The nature of the dangers associated with and the indicator signs of overtrading and overcapitalisation

The relationship between cash flow accounting and accounting for income and expenditure

Although this Unit is primarily concerned with cash flows for an organisation learners need to understand how cash flow accounting relates to accounting (financial) statements which are prepared to show the income and expenditure (profitability) of an organisation. Financial statements are prepared using accounting adjustments such as accruals, prepayments and depreciation and therefore do not show the cash position of an organisation. Information required for the preparation of a cash budget comes from a variety of sources which may include an Income Statement (Profit and Loss Account). Knowledge of how figures from financial accounting statements can be adjusted to reverse the effect of accounting adjustments and thereby find the cash transactions to be included in a cash budget is essential.

Cash flow statements prepared under FRS 1 are not assessable in this Unit.

Through practical tasks, learners should be able to demonstrate and understand:

- The difference between cash flow accounting and accounting for income and expenditure and the importance of distinguishing cash from profit

- How the value of cash transactions can be calculated by adjusting figures in the Income Statement to reverse the effect of accounting adjustments such as accruals, prepayments and depreciation

Cash receipts, cash payments and the likely pattern of cash flows

Effective liquidity management depends upon understanding that cash receipts and payments can be categorised in a number of ways according to their main characteristics and their differing patterns of cash flow. A cash budget needs to recognise different types of receipts and payments and incorporate a variety of payment patterns that arise both from the nature of the receipt or payment and from the effects of lagging.

In order to be able to determine the likely pattern of cash flows over a period it is necessary to understand the possible sources of information within an organisation and to recognise that transactions may be recorded in different ways in different parts of the organisation.

Through practical tasks, learners should be able to demonstrate they understand:

- The characteristics of regular, capital and exceptional cash receipts and give examples for each type of cash flow. Regular (operational) receipts are those that are expected to occur frequently and arise from the operating activities of the organisation. Capital receipts are those relating to proceeds from the disposal of non-current assets (fixed assets). Exceptional receipts are those that are not expected to recur on a regular basis and do not arise from the operating activities of the organisation however they could be large and thus materially impact the cash position of an organisation.

- The characteristics of regular, capital and exceptional cash payments as well as drawings and give examples for each type of cash flow. Regular (operational) cash payments are those that are expected to occur frequently and arise from the operating activities of the organisation. Capital payments relate to the acquisition of non-current assets. Exceptional payments are those that are not expected to recur on a regular basis and drawings are amounts withdrawn from the organisation by its owners, and could be either regular or irregular in nature. Exceptional items and irregular drawings could materially impact the cash position of the organisation.

- How recording and accounting practices may vary in different parts of the organisation resulting in a variety of sources of information being available for determining likely patterns of cash flow.

- The effect of lagged receipts and payments on an organisations cash flow and cash management.

- How to use information obtained from a range of sources within an organisation to determine the likely pattern of different types of cash receipts and cash payments for inclusion in a cash budget. Given the potential impact of exceptional receipts and payments on the cash position of an organisation, these types of cash flows should be anticipated to ensure that they are included in the cash budget in the correct period so that their likely effect can be assessed.

- How to determine the likely pattern of cash receipts and payments incorporating the effects of lagging.

Forecasting future cash receipts and payments

Known income and expenditure trends must be considered and incorporated into estimates of future cash receipts and payments that are to be included in a cash budget. There are a variety of statistical techniques that could be used to forecast future cash receipts and payments but this Unit focuses on moving averages and allowance for inflation. Previous income and expenditure trends could also be derived from graphical information or a review of historical results where this indicates simple, regular increases or decreases. Learners must be able to use these techniques to forecast future cash receipts and payments.

Through practical tasks, learners should be able to demonstrate they understand:

- How moving averages (time series analysis) can be used to identify past trends in volume or value which can then be used to estimate future trends

- How to use moving averages to identify the basic trend of income or expenditure and use this trend to forecast future cash receipts and payments. Calculations will be based on odd-points (i.e. 3-point, 5-point etc) only and therefore calculations including centred averages will not be required. Learners should be able to calculate period variations (seasonal variations) by finding the difference between the trend and the actual figure and use this to forecast income or expenditure. Any variations will be cyclical

- How to forecast future cash receipts and payments based on known trends by calculating and using an average monthly change

- A trend from graphical information and use the trend to forecast future cash receipts and payments

- The need to make allowances for inflation and describe the techniques that could be applied when estimating future trends of income and expenditure, for example the application of percentage increases and the use of index numbers

- How to forecast future cash receipts and payments making allowances for known trends in inflation

- The inherent problems of forecasting figures and how these can impact on the usefulness of a cash budget

Prepare cash budgets and indicate the net cash position

Cash budgets provide decision makers with an effective tool for cash management therefore learners who are able to accurately prepare a cash budget from a variety of information will be equipped with a valuable practical skill.

The preparation of a cash budget will necessarily require learners to use a range of information presented in a variety of ways depending upon the nature of the organisation and its activities. At this level learners will be expected to be able to extract information from data that is presented in different ways. However, clear instructions will be provided in assessment tasks so that a detailed knowledge of the preparation of budgets (other than cash), the composition of financial statements or the specific structure of an organisation will not be required.

Cash budgets are prepared using assumptions about the nature of cash flows. It is important to understand that net cash requirements will be affected by changes in those assumptions and that revised cash budgets will need to be prepared.

Through practical tasks, learners should be able to demonstrate they understand:

- The component parts of cash budgets. Cash budgets do not have a statutory format and organisations may chose to present information in different ways but for a cash budget to be useful it should incorporate the following:

  - Analysis of sources of receipts leading to total receipts for the period

  - Analysis of the sources of payments leading to total payments for the period

  - Net cash flow for the period

  - Bank balance bought forward

  - Bank balance carried forward

- The uses of a cash budget and explain how the format of a cash budget can aid decision making by showing the composition and timing of receipts and payments and changes in the net cash position

- How to calculate sales receipts for inclusion in a cash budget after accounting for early settlement discounts, sales price fluctuations, bad debts and the effect of lagging

- How to calculate purchase payments for inclusion in a cash budget after accounting for early settlement discounts, purchase price fluctuations and the effect of lagging

- How to calculate non-sales receipts and non-purchase payments for inclusion in the cash budget from a variety of information incorporating different payment patterns. Clear instructions will be given in the assessment data regarding the payment pattern of these types of cash flows

- How to prepare a cash budget for a number of periods for a new or an existing organisation, clearly indicating the net cash position at the end of each period. Cash budget figures should be rounded to whole £'s following normal rounding conventions

- How to calculate and incorporate bank interest received and bank interest paid into a cash budget

- How to prepare revised cash budgets to quantify changes in the net cash requirements that result when original assumptions regarding volumes, values and payment patterns change

Anticipate and manage cash shortages by raising suitable finance

A cash budget is one method that an organisation can use to anticipate future cash shortages based on their forecast activities. A cash budget provides a periodic forecast of net cash positions that will enable management to select and arrange suitable financing options to cover any cash shortages.

Organisations can raise finance from a range of sources but this Unit only requires knowledge of finance raised from banks in the form of overdrafts and loans. Learners need to understand that all financing options have differing terms and conditions attached to them and that there are a number of factors that need to be considered before recommending a suitable form of finance. Different organisations may have established regulations, policies and guidelines governing the sources of, and terms under which, finance can be raised. An important point to recognise is that those charged with liquidity management owe a fiduciary duty of care to the owners of the organisation.

Through practical tasks, learners should be able to demonstrate they understand:

- Statutory and other organisational regulations and guidelines that relate to the management of cash balances. Learners will not be expected to identify specific statutory regulations but must be aware that some organisations are governed by mandatory regulations that need to be adhered to e.g. limited companies through the Companies Act, and public sector organisations

- Financing can be obtained from banks in the form of loans and overdrafts

- The main features of overdrafts and loans available from a bank, including interest rates (fixed, variable and capped), fees, time period, repayment structure, security (personal guarantee, fixed and floating charges), advantages and disadvantages. Explain the nature, purpose and content of facility letters

- How to use a cash budget to anticipate financing requirements and arrange overdraft and loan facilities on the most favourable terms available

- What is required in order to make recommendations for financing cash shortfalls identified by a cash budget, selecting the most appropriate form of financing for a particular project considering the time period, purpose and amount of finance needed. Recommendations should consider the possibility of combining different types of financing options to maintain an adequate level of liquidity at the lowest possible cost and to meet the organisation's own guidelines and regulations

Use forecasts to monitor cash flow within an organisation, identify significant variations and take corrective action

In addition to being a tool for predicting cash shortfalls and cash surpluses, a cash budget can be used to monitor and control cash inflows and outflows. Cash management is not simply about being able to prepare a cash budget it also involves being able to quantify deviations from budget and to identify possible reasons for those deviations so that appropriate courses of action can be taken.

Through practical tasks, learners should be able to demonstrate they understand:

- Compare actual cash flows with forecast cash flows to calculate deviations (variances). Standard costing variance analysis is not assessable at this level.

- Summarise deviations from cash budget by reconciling budgeted cash flow with actual cash flow.

- Identify possible reasons for differences between budgeted cash flows and actual cash flows (both adverse and favourable) so that corrective action can be suggested. Recommended action must have regard to the impact of such actions on the cash position of the organisation and on organisational policies. Ensure that possible courses of action are matched with the nature and cause of cash variances.

Managing surplus funds

As well as being able to select suitable finance for dealing with cash shortages organisations need to utilise cash surpluses in the most appropriate manner to ensure that they receive maximum return for minimum risk. Different organisations have different regulations and guidelines governing investment and learners must take these into account when making recommendations.

Through practical tasks, learners should be able to demonstrate they understand:

- What is meant by the term 'treasury function'

- Explain how the government's monetary policy in controlling the supply of money in the economy,

- and the effect of this on the rate of inflation and interest rates, impacts an organisations treasury function

- That different organisations will have their own financial regulations, guidelines and security procedures (including physical security) that must be observed when considering possible courses of action and making recommendations. Describe how these regulations, guidelines and procedures affect the organisations principles of cash management

- Different types of investments and the nature, risks, cost, terms and conditions associated with them including certificates of deposit, government securities, local authority short term loans and shares

- Ways that an organisation could manage risk and exposure when investing surplus funds to try and ensure that potential losses are minimised

- What is required in order to make recommendations for investing surplus funds having regard to the organisations policies and procedures, internal regulations, attitude towards risk, return, termination costs, realisation and authorisation limits

THE ASSESSMENT

The format of the assessment

The assessment will be divided into two sections.

Section 1 covers:

- Preparing a cash budget

- Recognising the importance of cash

- Relationship between cash and profit

- Forecasting income and expenditure using a variety of techniques

There are four tasks in this section

Section 2 covers:

- Skills needed to manage cash balances in accordance with organisationsal guidelines

- Sensitivity analysis

- Cash flow monitoring

- Raising finance

- Investing surplus funds

There are four tasks in this section

Learners will normally be assessed by computer based assessment (CBA), which will include extended writing tasks, and will be required to demonstrate competence in both sections of the assessment.

Time allowed

The time allowed for this assessment is **120 minutes.**

STUDY SKILLS

Preparing to study

Devise a study plan

Determine which times of the week you will study.

Split these times into sessions of at least one hour for study of new material. Any shorter periods could be used for revision or practice.

Put the times you plan to study onto a study plan for the weeks from now until the assessment and set yourself targets for each period of study – in your sessions make sure you cover the whole course, activities and the associated questions in the workbook at the back of the manual.

If you are studying more than one unit at a time, try to vary your subjects as this can help to keep you interested and see subjects as part of wider knowledge.

When working through your course, compare your progress with your plan and, if necessary, re-plan your work (perhaps including extra sessions) or, if you are ahead, do some extra revision / practice questions.

Effective studying

Active reading

You are not expected to learn the text by rote, rather, you must understand what you are reading and be able to use it to pass the assessment and develop good practice.

A good technique is to use SQ3Rs – Survey, Question, Read, Recall, Review:

1   **Survey the chapter**

    Look at the headings and read the introduction, knowledge, skills and content, so as to get an overview of what the chapter deals with.

2   **Question**

    Whilst undertaking the survey ask yourself the questions you hope the chapter will answer for you.

3   Read

Read through the chapter thoroughly working through the activities and, at the end, making sure that you can meet the learning objectives highlighted on the first page.

4   Recall

At the end of each section and at the end of the chapter, try to recall the main ideas of the section / chapter without referring to the text. This is best done after short break of a couple of minutes after the reading stage.

5   Review

Check that your recall notes are correct.

You may also find it helpful to re-read the chapter to try and see the topic(s) it deals with as a whole.

Note taking

Taking notes is a useful way of learning, but do not simply copy out the text.

The notes must:

- be in your own words
- be concise
- cover the key points
- well organised
- be modified as you study further chapters in this text or in related ones.

Trying to summarise a chapter without referring to the text can be a useful way of determining which areas you know and which you don't.

Three ways of taking notes

1   Summarise the key points of a chapter

2   Make linear notes

A list of headings, subdivided with sub-headings listing the key points.

If you use linear notes, you can use different colours to highlight key points and keep topic areas together.

Use plenty of space to make your notes easy to use.

3 Try a diagrammatic form

The most common of which is a mind map.

To make a mind map, put the main heading in the centre of the paper and put a circle around it.]

Draw lines radiating from this to the main sub-headings which again have circles around them.

Continue the process from the sub-headings to sub-sub-headings.

Highlighting and underlining

You may find it useful to underline or highlight key points in your study text – but do be selective.

You may also wish to make notes in the margins.

Revision phase

Kaplan has produced material specifically designed for your final examination preparation for this unit.

These include pocket revision notes and a bank of revision questions specifically in the style of the new syllabus.

Further guidance on how to approach the final stage of your studies is given in these materials.

Further reading

In addition to this text, you should also read the "Student section" of the "Accounting Technician" magazine every month to keep abreast of any guidance from the examiners.

Terminology for CMGT

There are different terms used to mean the same thing – you will need to be aware of both sets of terminology.

UK GAAP	IAS
Profit and Loss	Income Statement
Sales	Revenue
Balance Sheet	Statement of Financial Position
Fixed Assets	Non-current Assets
Current Assets	Property, Plant and Equipment
Stock	Inventory
Trade Debtors	Trade Receivables
Trade Creditors	Trade Payables
Capital	Equity
Profit	Retained Earnings

Liquidity

1

Introduction

This chapter demonstrates how important cash is to a business. It looks at liquidity and how cash differs to profit. It also looks at the issues of over trading and over capitalisation.

KNOWLEDGE	CONTENTS
Describe the relationship between cash flow accounting and accounting for income and expenditure (3.3) Identify the principles of liquidity management (3.4)	1 Liquidity 2 Cash flow and profit 3 Working capital cycle

1 Liquidity

1.1 Liquidity

Liquidity in the business means **having enough cash or ready access to cash to meet all payment obligations when these fall due**. The main sources of liquidity are usually:

- cash in the bank
- short term investments that can be cashed in easily and quickly
- cash inflows from normal trading operations (cash sales and payments by receivables for credit sales)
- an overdraft facility or other ready source of extra borrowing

1.2 What is cash?

Cash in this unit is used to include bank accounts as well as coins and notes and cash payments include cheque payments, BACS, direct debits and standing orders.

2 Cash flow and profit

2.1 The importance of cash flow

Any business will wish to make a profit. This means that over a period of time sales made are worth more than the cost of making those sales together with the expenses incurred by the business. However, even if the business is making a profit, it must also have the cash available to pay its suppliers, pay its employees and pay for its expenses.

It is entirely possible for a profitable business to run short of cash. For example, a business may be making a profit but it has to replace a large item of machinery and this will deplete its cash resources to the extent that it may not be able to pay its creditors when they fall due. In the worst case scenario this might even mean that the business is forced into liquidation.

2.2 The difference between cash flow and profit

There are a variety of reasons why the profit of a business will not necessarily equate directly to cash inflows:

- **Revenue** is recognised in the profit and loss account when it is earned but not when the cash is received (accruals concept).

- **Costs** are recognised in the profit and loss account when it is incurred but not when the cash is paid (accruals concept).

- **Non-cash expenses** – the profit and loss account of a business is charged with a number of non-cash expenses such as **depreciation** and **provisions for doubtful debts**. Although these are correctly charged as expenses in the profit and loss account, they are not cash flows and will not reduce the cash balance of the business.

- **Purchase of fixed assets** – these are often large cash outflows of a business but the only amount that is charged to the profit and loss account is the annual depreciation charge not the entire cost of the fixed asset.

- **Sale of fixed assets** – when a fixed asset is sold this will result in an inflow of cash to the business but the figure to appear in the profit and loss account is not the sales proceeds but any profit or loss on the sale.

- **Financing transactions** – some transactions, such as issuing additional share capital and taking out or repaying a loan, will result in large cash flows in or out of the business with no effect on the profit figure at all.

2.3 Accruals concept

One major reason for there being a difference between cash flow and profit is that the profit is calculated in the profit and loss account by applying the accruals concept.

🔍 Definition

FRS 18 *Accounting Policies* defines the accruals concept as follows.

'The accruals basis of accounting requires the non-cash effects of transactions and other events to be reflected, as far as is possible, in the financial statements for the accounting period in which they occur and not, for example, in the period in which any cash involved is received or paid.'

The accruals basis of accounting covers the accounting for all income and expenditure but the differences that it causes between profit and cash flow are probably best illustrated for sales and purchases.

Example

Jan set up in business selling computer accessories on 1 March 20Y1 with cash in her bank account of £10,000. During the first month of trading she purchased £4,000 of goods on credit and sold them all on credit for £6,000. She is due to pay for the purchases on 15 April 20Y1 and her customers are due to pay for the goods they have bought on 30 April.

What is her profit for the month of March and what is her cash flow?

Solution

Under the accruals concept the profit that would be reported would be the sales actually made during the month and the cost of making those sales.

	£
Sales	6,000
Cost of sales	(4,000)
Profit	2,000

However, as she has neither paid for the purchases nor received money for the sales, she has had no cash flow during the month.

The accruals concept therefore is one major reason for the difference between reported profit and cash flow. As well as applying to sales and purchases, the concept requires accruals and prepayments of expenses to be recognised at the end of a period.

2.4 Closing stock

The accruals concept also applies to the accounting treatment of any stocks remaining at the end of a period when calculating the profit for the period. The sales for the period are compared to the cost of selling those goods so any unsold goods, the closing stock, are carried forward to the following period by being deducted from the purchases figure.

Example

Ken set up in business selling flat pack furniture on 1 June 20Y1 when he had £20,000 in his bank account. During the month of June he purchased furniture for cash of £7,000 and sold most of this on credit for £10,000. The debtors are not due to pay until 16 July. At the end of June the cost of the furniture that he had left was £1,500.

What is Ken's profit for the month of June and what is his cash flow?

Solution

Under the accruals concept not only will the sales appear in the profit calculation even though no cash has been received for them during the month but the purchases figures will be reduced by the cost of the goods not yet sold so that the sales figure is matched with the cost of the actual goods sold.

	£	£
Sales		10,000
Purchases	7,000	
Less: Closing stock	(1,500)	
	————	
Cost of sales		5,500
		————
Profit		4,500
		————

The cash flow of the business, however, is simply the cash spent on the purchases so although the profit appears as £4,500, the cash outflow is £7,000 leaving him with just £13,000 in his bank account at the end of the month.

3 Working capital cycle

3.1 Working capital

 Definition

Working capital is the short-term net assets of the business made up of stock, debtors, creditors and cash.

Working capital is the capital available for conducting the day to day operations of an organisation. It is normally expressed as the excess of current assets over current liabilities.

Working capital management is the management of all aspects of both current assets and current liabilities, to minimise the risk of insolvency while maximising the return on assets.

3.2 Working capital cycle

The working capital cycle or the **cash operating cycle** is the length of time between the company's outlay on raw materials, wages and other expenditures and the inflow of cash from the sale of goods. The faster a firm can 'push' items around the cycle the lower its investment in working capital will

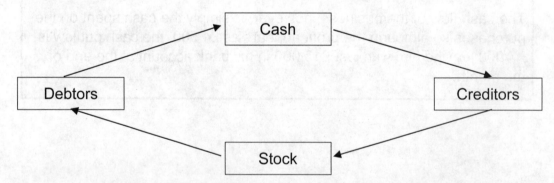

The length of the cycle depends on how the balancing act between liquidity and profitability is resolved, the efficiency of management and the nature of the industry. The optimum level is the amount that results in no idle cash or unused inventory, but that does not put a strain on liquid resources. Trying to shorten the cash cycle may have detrimental effects elsewhere, with the organisation lacking the cash to meet its commitments and losing sales since customers will generally prefer to buy from suppliers who are prepared to extend trade credit, and who have items available when required.

Additionally, any assessment of the acceptability or otherwise of the length of the cycle must take into account the nature of the business involved. A supermarket chain will tend to have a very low or negative cycle – they have very few, if any, credit customers, they have a high inventory turnover and they can negotiate quite long credit periods with their suppliers.

3.3 Calculating the cycle

The working capital cycle can be calculated in days, weeks or months using the following formulas:

Debtor days

$$\text{Average collection period} = \frac{\text{debtors}}{\text{credit sales}} \times 365$$

Creditor days

$$\text{Average collection period} = \frac{\text{creditors}}{\text{credit purchases}} \times 365$$

Stock holding days

$$\text{Average holding period} = \frac{\text{stock}}{\text{cost of sales}} \times 365$$

Note : in some instances it may not be possible to locate the figures for credit sales or credit purchase in which case the next best item is used i.e. sales, turnover or revenue for debtor days and purchases or cost of sales for creditor days.

For CMGT you will not need to calculate the individual formulas but you will need to use the following to calculate the length of the working capital cycle:

Stock holding period + Debtor days – Creditor days

Example

Below are the relevant details from the balance sheet and profit and loss account from Josh Plc. Calculate the working capital cycle.

Balance sheet

	£000	£000
Current assets		
Stocks	500	
Debtors	1,000	
Balance at bank	200	
	1,700	
Creditors: Amounts falling due within one year	(900)	
		800

Profit and Loss account

	£000
Turnover	5,000
Cost of sales	(3,000)
Gross profit	2,000
Operating expenses	(500)
Net profit	1,500

Stock holding days $= \dfrac{\text{stock}}{\text{cost of sales}} \times 365 = \dfrac{500}{3,000} \times 365 = 60.8$ days

Debtor days $= \dfrac{\text{debtors}}{\text{credit sales}} \times 365 = \dfrac{1,000}{5,000} \times 365 = 73$ days

Creditor days $= \dfrac{\text{creditors}}{\text{credit purchases}} \times 365 = \dfrac{900}{3,000} \times 365 = 109.5$ days

Working capital cycle = 60.8 + 73 − 109.5 = 24.3 days

Activity 1

A business has an average stock holding period of 100 days, received payment from its customers in 60 days and pays its creditors in 80 days. What is the cash operating cycle in days for the business?

A   120 days

B   80 days

C   40 days

D   240 days

3.1   Overtrading

Overtrading usually occurs when a company tries to **expand too quickly** and **over-stretches its working capital** due to inadequate financing for its growth rate. If **sales increase too rapidly**, then working capital requirements may increase as **more money is tied up in stocks** of raw materials to support the increased sales levels; **debtors will also rise**. This can lead to a situation in which the company is operating at a profit but suffers a liquidity crisis as it has insufficient cash to pay its bills and expenses.

This problem happens over a period of time, with the working capital gradually being stretched and without the managers of the company realising what is happening as the company continues to be profitable. The balance sheet eventually reveals the problem.

3.2   Identifying signs of overtrading

Signs of overtrading can be identified as follows:

- sharply and rapidly increasing sales volumes
- falling profit margins despite increased sales as higher discounts are given to attract more customers and production costs increase due to overtime costs, etc
- greater reliance on short-term funding such as overdrafts
- longer debtor/creditor collection ratios.

3.3   Controlling overtrading

Planned overtrading is not dangerous; it is the unmanaged and undetected overtrading that causes company downfalls.

If, however, the symptoms of unmanaged overtrading are detected, then the problem may be averted by:

- issuing new share capital or loan stock

- taking out long-term loans rather than overdrafts

- reducing the operating cycle by controlling debtors and creditors

- slowing down the company's expansion.

3.4   Over-capitalisation

The opposite of overtrading is over-capitalisation. There is too much cash. Consequently profit is suppressed in relation to the capital investment in the company and earnings per £ of capital are low. Unless this surplus can be invested by the company to earn a good return, it could be distributed to shareholders through a higher dividend or a buyback of shares.

 Activity 2

Overtrading can occur when working capital levels are too high.

True or false?

Over-capitalisation can occur when working capital levels are too low.

True or false?

Which of the following are signs of overtrading?

A   Rapidly decreasing sales volumes

B   Rapidly increasing sales volumes

C   Increased profit margins

D   Falling profit margins

E   Short debtor collection periods

F   Longer debtor collection periods

G   Shorter creditor payment periods

H   Longer creditor payment periods

I   Greater reliance on short term funding

J   Less reliance on short term funding

---

4 Summary

This chapter demonstrates how important cash and liquidity is to a business. The amount of cash a business has is not the same as the profit made due to the accruals concept.

Poor working capital management can lead to either issues of over trading or over capitalisation.

 Test your knowledge

Having completed Chapter 1 you should now be able to attempt:

Practice Activities 1 to 5

Answers to chapter activities

Activity 1

Answer B

100 + 60 – 80 = 80 days

Activity 2

Overtrading can occur when working capital levels are too high.

False

Over-capitalisation can occur when working capital levels are too low.

False

Which of the following are signs of overtrading?

B   Rapidly increasing sales volumes

D   Falling profit margins

F   Longer debtor collection periods

H   Longer creditor payment periods

I   Greater reliance on short term funding

Cash budgets

2

Introduction

In this chapter we will consider the importance of cash flow to a business and the typical types of cash flows that a business will have. From this, the chapter moves on to the methods of preparing a cash budget or cash flow forecast for a business.

KNOWLEDGE	CONTENTS
Explain how recording and accounting practices may vary in different parts of the organisation (1.2)	1 Cash flows
	2 Types of cash flows
Identify the characteristics of the main types of cash receipts and payment of: regular revenue receipt; capital receipts; exceptional receipts and payments; drawings (2.1)	3 Preparation of cash budgets
	4 Receipts
	5 Payments
Identify the component parts of cash budgets and how these are presented to aid decision making (3.1)	6 Profit and loss adjustments
	7 Worked example
Explain the effects f lagged receipts and payments upon an organisation's cash management (3.2)	

SKILLS

Determine the likely pattern of cash flow over the accounting period, and anticipate any exceptional receipts or payments (1.1)

Prepare cash budgets and clearly indicate net cash requirements (1.3)

1 Cash flows

1.1 The importance of cash flow

Cash is a business's most important asset as without cash it is not possible to pay for the running of the business. Managers must forecast and monitor cash flows to ensure the business does not become bankrupt.

Cash budgets are prepared:

- To show when cash surpluses are likely to occur
- To show when large and unusually items can be paid for
- To show where there is inadequate cash to finance any plans
- To act as an indicator of when extra finance will be needed
- To provide a basis of control for the forthcoming year
- Centrally, as this eliminates duplication of 'buffer stock' of cash and allows cross subsidisation of divisions.

2 Types of cash flows

2.1 Introduction

We must now start to focus on the different types of cash flow that a business is likely to have. Some will be regular receipts and payments such as sales, purchases and expenses. Some will be receipts and payments of a long-term nature, known as capital receipts and payments such as the raising of share capital or the purchase of fixed assets. Some payments will be made to the owners of a business either in the form of drawings for a sole trader or partnership or dividends for a company. There will also be necessary disbursements such as the payment of taxes to the government. Finally, there may be unusual or exceptional receipts or payments, for example for cash received from the sale of a fixed asset.

Every business will have different types of receipts and payments and different patterns of those receipts and payments but we will consider the typical types of cash flows that you may come across.

2.2 Cash inflows

Revenue receipts for a business will be cash sales and cash from debtors who have purchased goods on credit. Capital receipts will include cash raised by issuing shares or raising a loan. Other types of capital cash inflow are the proceeds from the sale of fixed assets or the receipt of government grants. These are not likely to be regular cash inflows.

2.3 Cash outflows

- Revenue payments will include payments for cash purchases, cash paid to creditors, wages payments, payment of bills, and cash payment of expenses.

- Capital payments could include the repayment of loans or the purchase of fixed assets. When new fixed assets are purchased this may be for a large sum on just one date or it may take the form of regular payments if, for example, the asset is acquired under a lease or hire purchase agreement.

- Businesses will also be likely to make payments or disbursements in the form of corporation tax, VAT and PAYE. These may be regular such as the monthly PAYE payments or one-off payments each year such as the annual payment of corporation tax.

- Payments will also be made to providers of finance such as dividends to shareholders and interest payments to banks and other providers of finance. The regularity of these payments will vary but, for example, companies usually pay any dividend twice a year, a small interim dividend during the year and a larger final dividend after the year end.

- Finally, in a sole trader's business or a partnership there may be either regular or irregular payments made to the owner or partners in the form of drawings.

2.4 Exceptional cash flows

The cash flows described above are the normal, everyday types of cash flows that most businesses will have. However in some cases there will also be exceptional cash flows which are not part of normal business operations. Exceptional cash outflows might include payment of legal damages or redundancy costs. Exceptional cash inflows might include items such as receipts from an insurance company for damaged stock.

Activity 1

Cash flows can be classified between regular revenue receipts and payments and infrequent or irregular receipts and disbursements. Complete the table by matching the correct description to the type of receipt or payment:

Regular revenue receipts	
Exceptional payments	
Capital payment	
Drawings	
Annual disbursement	

Options:

A   Payments that relate to the proceeds from the disposal of fixed assets

B   Payments that relate to the acquisition of fixed assets

C   Payments made to the owners of the business

D   Payments received from the owners of the business

E   Income received from HM Revenue and Customs

F   Income received from the operating activities of the business that are expected to occur frequently

G   Payments arising from the operating activities of the business that are expected to occur frequently

H   Payments that do not arise from the operating activities of the business and that not are expected to occur frequently

I   Payment made to HM Revenue and Customs

3 Preparation of cash budgets

3.1   Cash budget

A cash budget or cash flow forecast is an **estimate of all of the cash inflows and all of the cash outflows for the period**. When these are applied to the opening cash figure, the closing estimated cash balance at the end of each period can be determined and management can plan to take any necessary action: for example agreement with the bank for an overdraft facility if the budgeted cash balance is negative or the arrangement for short-term investment if the cash balance is budgeted to be healthy.

We will look at the detailed preparation of cash budgets by looking at the main elements individually and then bringing it all together in a full-scale worked example.

Cash budgets are not difficult to produce but in an assessment you will often find that a lot of information has to be absorbed and used, which can be daunting. A logical approach is what is required.

3.2 Proforma receipts and payments cash budget

Cash budget for the three months to September 20X4

	July £	Aug £	Sept £
RECEIPTS			
Cash sales			
Cash from debtors			
Capital introduced			
Total receipts			
PAYMENTS			
Fixed costs			
Payments to creditors			
Purchases of fixed assets			
Total payments			
Net cash flow			
Opening bank balance			
Closing bank balance			

Each cash budget has to be **amended to reflect** the particular circumstances of the business.

For example, businesses with only cash sales will not need the line for cash from debtors. Also, other sources of income may arise, such as proceeds from the sale of fixed assets. There are many sorts of cash payments; possibly cash purchases as well as credit purchases, wages and salaries to employees or the drawings of a proprietor, and each must be detailed line by line under the payments heading.

The crucial point to remember is that all cash inflows and all cash outflows over the budget period must be considered. As you work through the following examples and questions, you will see examples of different receipts and payments but note how the basic proforma above is used to find the net cash balance.

Example

At 1 March 20X4 Apple Ltd expects to have a bank balance of £2,000. It is estimated that cash from sales in March, April and May will be £24,000 each month. Cash payments for expenses each month are estimated to be £21,000 but in May some new equipment must be purchased at a cost of £12,000 paid for on 1 May by cheque.

Prepare the cash budget for the next three months and determine the net cash position at the end of each of the three months.

Solution

Cash budget	March £	April £	May £
Cash inflows	24,000	24,000	24,000
Cash outflows:			
Expenses	(21,000)	(21,000)	(21,000)
Capital expenditure			(12,000)
Net cash inflow/(outflow)	3,000	3,000	(9,000)
Opening cash balance	2,000	5,000	8,000
Closing cash balance	5,000	8,000	(1,000)

The closing cash balance at the end of each month is derived by adding or deducting the net cash flow for the month to or from the cash balance at the start of the month. The closing cash balance of one month therefore becomes the opening cash balance the following month.

This indicates to management that although there will be cash in the bank at the end of March and April, there is expected to be a shortage at the end of May. Management can then use this information to plan for this eventuality by, for example, arranging for a bank overdraft or bank loan or selling some surplus assets.

4 Receipts

4.1 Introduction

There are a number of ways that a business can receive cash – through day to day trading, through accessing finance (loan) or from interest received on an investment.

4.2 Sales receipts

Sales are often made on credit and customers do not pay until subsequent periods. The credit terms offered to customers will be decided by the managers and a general pattern of receipts from these customers can therefore be established. The cash budget needs to show when the actual cash is expected to be received from debtors in the period rather than the actual sales made to debtors in the period.

Example

A business makes sales on credit and cash. The cash accounts for 20% of the sales and the remaining 80% relates to the sales on credit. We need to state cash receipts for the first three months of the year. Of these cash receipts 60% are received in the month of sale and 40% in the month after sale.

Solution

	Dec £	Jan £	Feb £	Mar £
Sales	10,000	12,000	14,000	16,000
Of which are:				
Cash	2,000	2,400	2,800	3,200
Credit	8,000	9,600	11,200	12,800
The cash receipts from the debtors will be:				
60% in month of sale	4,800	5,760	6,720	7,680
40% in subsequent month	–	3,200	3,840	4,480
Giving:				
Total cash receipts	6,800	11,360	13,360	15,360

The above example shows how payments from debtors for a particular month are not the same as sales to debtors for that month.

4.3 Sales on credit and discounts

In some businesses a cash or settlement discount is offered to customers for payment within a certain time period. This means that although the cash is received sooner, a lower amount is received than was invoiced. This must be taken into account when preparing the cash budget.

> **Example**
>
> A business offers a 3% discount for payment received from credit customers in the month of sale. The business has found that 40% of customers take advantage of this by paying in the month of sale, 50% of customers pay in the month after the sale and 10% of customers pay two months after the month of sale.
>
> Credit sales for the business are as follows:
>
> | | Actual | | | Budgeted | |
> |---|---|---|---|---|---|
> | | *February* | *March* | *April* | *May* | *June* |
> | | £ | £ | £ | £ | £ |
> | Credit sales | 20,000 | 22,000 | 24,000 | 18,000 | 21,000 |
>
> **Solution**
>
> | | *April* | *May* | *June* |
> |---|---|---|---|
> | | £ | £ | £ |
> | Sales | 24,000 | 18,000 | 21,000 |
>
> The cash receipts from the debtors will be:
>
> | | | | |
> |---|---|---|---|
> | 40% in month of sale less 3% discount | 9,312 | 6,984 | 8,148 |
> | 50% in subsequent month | 11,000* | 12,000 | 9,000 |
> | 10% two months after sale | 2,000** | 2,200** | 2,400** |
>
> Giving:
>
> | | | | |
> |---|---|---|---|
> | Total cash receipts | 22,312 | 21,184 | 19,548 |
>
> * March 22,000 × 50%** February 20,000 × 10%; March 22,000 ×10%; April 24,000 × 10%

4.4 Bad debts

It is also entirely possible that some debts will become bad debts. This means that the cash will never be received from these debtors. Therefore the amounts due from these debtors must not be included in the cash budget as it is likely that the cash will never be received.

Example

A business offers a 2% discount for payment received from credit customers in the month of sale. The business has found that 30% of customers take advantage of this by paying in the month of sale, 40% of customers pay in the month after the sale and 20% of customers pay two months after the month of sale. From past experience it is known that 10% of the customers do not pay.

Credit sales for the business are as follows:

	Actual			Budgeted	
	February £	March £	April £	May £	June £
Credit sales	10,000	20,000	30,000	25,000	30,000

Solution

	April £	May £	June £
Sales	30,000	25,000	30,000

The cash receipts from the debtors will be:

30% in month of sale less 2% discount	8,820	7,350	8,820
40% in subsequent month	8,000*	12,000	10,000
20% two months after sale	2,000**	4,000**	6,000**
10% bad debt	0	0	0

Giving:

Total cash receipts	18,820	23,350	24,820

* March 20,000 × 40%** February 10,000 × 20%; March 20,000 ×20%; April 30,000 × 20%

Bad debts are not recovered therefore no cash is received

4.5 Sales quantities and prices

In the examples so far you have been given the monetary amount of the sales in each month in order to calculate the receipts from debtors. However, you may be given information about the sales quantity in units each month and the selling price per unit. From this, the total monetary amount of the sales for the month can be calculated.

Activity 2

Kelly Limited sold 3,000 units of its only product in June 20X3 at a selling price of £45 each. Owing to an increase in production costs, this price increases to £48 with effect from 1 July 20X3 and this is expected to reduce demand for July to 2,900 units. Thereafter, however, demand is expected to increase by 10% per month.

Cash sales account for 500 units per month and are expected to remain at this level. Credit sales account for the balance and debtors pay as follows:

(a)   60% by value in the month of sale, receiving a 2% discount

(b)   40% by value in the following month.

Credit sales in May were £103,500

What are the budgeted cash receipts in June, July and August 20X3?

	June £	July £	Aug £
Sales units	3000	2900	3190
Selling price per unit	45	48	48
Sales	135000	139200	153120
Of which are:	22500 ✓	24000 ✓	24000 ✓
Cash 3000−500 x .06	60% 67500	69120	7 7472
Credit 3000 − 5000 x .04	40% 32400	45000	46080 ✓
The cash receipts from the debtors will be:			
In month of sale	22500	24000	24000
In subsequent month	66150	67738	75923
Giving:			
Total cash receipts			

4.6   Interest received

One of the purposes of a cash budget is to identify the cash balance at the end of each month and to determine whether any interest is due to the business from the bank.

In practice the amount of the interest will be calculated on a daily basis. However for cash budgeting purposes the amount of interest will normally be calculated on the basis of the amount of the credit balance at the end of the previous month. This figure for interest will then be included in the following month's cash receipts.

Example

A business anticipates having a credit balance of £2,000 at the end of March. The budgeted cash receipts and payments (excluding interest) for the following three months are expected to be as follows:

	April £	May £	June £
Cash receipts	16,500	18,000	17,200
Cash payments	17,400	17,500	17,000

Interest is charged at 0.5% per month on the basis of the positive balance at the start of each month.

Prepare the completed cash budget including the amount of interest.

Solution

		April £	May £	June £
Cash receipts		16,500	18,000	17,200
interest	(2,000 × 0.5%)	10		
	(1,110 × 0.5%)		6	
	(1,616 × 0.5%)			8
Cash payments		(17,400)	(17,500)	(17,000)
Net cash flow		(890)	506	208
Opening balance		2,000	1,110	1,616
Closing balance		1,110	1,616	1,824

4.7 Sale of assets

If a business sells an asset it will receive cash for the asset. This cash is classed as an inflow.

Be careful to include the actual cash received for the sale of the asset and not the profit or loss on sale.

5 Payments

5.1 Payments to creditors

The calculation for payments made to creditors is similar to that for receipts from debtors – you will be told the amount of credit purchases and the payment pattern to creditors. There may be the offer of a discount on payments as well for early payment.

 Example

A business estimates that its credit purchases for February and March will be £14,000 but will increase by 10% each month thereafter. Its payment pattern to creditors is that 60% are paid in the month following the purchases and the remaining 40% two months after the purchase.

What are the payments to creditors for the three months of March, April and May?

Solution

	February £	March £	April £	May £
Purchases (increasing by 10% each month)	14,000	14,000	15,400	16,940
Payments to creditors				
One month after purchase		8,400	8,400	9,240
Two months after purchase			5,600	5,600
Cash payments		8,400	14,000	14,840

Activity 3

Remus's purchases in May were £100,000 and these are expected to increase by £10,000 per month for the next three months. 30% of purchases are for cash, the balance being credit purchases. Creditors are paid as follows:

(a) 50% in the month of purchase (this qualifies for a 5% discount)

(b) 30% in the month after purchase

(c) 20% two months after purchase.

What is the cash outflow for July and August?

	May £	June £	July £	Aug £
Purchases	100,000	110,000	120,000	130,000
Payments to creditors				
Cash	30,000	33000	36000	39000
In the month of purchase	15,	104500	114000	123500
One month after purchase	30	33000	6000	31000
Two months after purchase	20,000	2000	2600	26000
Cash payments				

5.2 Purchases expressed in terms of sales value

In some cases the information supplied about purchases will be expressed in terms of the sales value which has been budgeted for i.e. sales figures will be provided together with the anticipated gross profit margin. The purchases each month will then be calculated using the gross profit percentage given to find the cost of purchases. Once the purchases are known then the cash payments to the suppliers can be calculated.

 Example

A business has the following budgeted sales:

	February £	March £	April £	May £	June £	July £
Budgeted sales	38,000	40,000	44,000	46,000	45,000	50,000

The business operates at a gross margin of 40% and its policy is to make purchases on credit each month which are enough to cover the following month's sales. Creditors are paid two months after the month of purchase. What are the payments to creditors for each of the four months of April, May, June and July?

Solution

The first step is to calculate the cost of purchases incurred in each month.

If there is a gross profit margin of 40% then purchases are 60% of sales.

	Feb £	March £	April £	May £	June £	July £
Budgeted sales	38,000	40,000	44,000	46,000	45,000	50,000
Purchases (60% of following month's sales)	24,000	26,400	27,600	27,000	30,000	

The next step is to apply the timing of the payment.

Payments (two months after purchase)			24,000	26,400	27,600	27,000

5.3 Increase or decrease in stock levels

Another method of expressing information about purchase quantities is to include plans for any increases or decreases in stock levels during the period. If stock levels are to be increased then purchases must be larger but if stock levels are budgeted to decrease then the amount of purchases will also decrease.

 Example

A business generally has purchases of £80,000 each month on credit. These are paid for in the month following the purchase. However, it is budgeted to increase stock levels at the end of May by £20,000 and that stock levels will then remain at that value. There is no anticipated increase in sales.

What are the cash payments to creditors for each of the three months of April, May and June?

Solution

Again the first step is to calculate the amount of purchases each month. This will generally be £80,000 but in May must be £100,000 in order to increase the stock levels. As there is no anticipated increase in sales levels then purchases in June can revert to £80,000.

	March £	April £	May £	June £
Purchases	80,000	80,000	100,000	80,000

As payments are made in the month following the purchase then the cash payments will be as follows:

	April £	May £	June £
Purchases	80,000	100,000	80,000

5.4 Cash budgets and manufacturing organisations

You will not be asked to prepare a cash budget within a manufacturing organisation but you need to be aware of them in order to determine payments to creditors.

(a) The production budget

The production budget is the amount of finished goods to be made in a period. This is calculated as follows:

		Units
Sales		X
Less:	Opening stock of finished goods	(X)
Add:	Closing stock of finished goods	X
Production		X

If finished goods stock levels remain constant then the quantity of production will be the same as that of sales, but if the stock levels are budgeted to change this will affect the amount of production.

(b) The purchases budget

Once the number of units that are to be produced each month has been determined then the amount of raw materials required to be purchased for that production can be determined. The amount to be purchased will depend upon any changes in raw materials stock levels and the purchases can be calculated as:

	Units
Raw materials required for production	X
Less:　Opening stock of raw materials	(X)
Add:　Closing stock of raw materials	X
Purchases	X

Take care not to confuse opening and closing stocks of finished goods and opening and closing stocks of raw materials. The finished goods stock levels are used to determine the production budget and the raw materials stock levels are used in the determination of the purchases budget.

(c) **The cash budget**

Finally the cost of these purchases and the payment pattern for these materials can be calculated. We have already seen that the cash paid to the creditor for purchases may lag the actual purchase by a number of months.

🔆 Example

A business has planned sales of its product of 4,000 units in March which will be expected to increase by 200 units each month. Finished goods stock at the start and end of March is anticipated to be 500 units and these are budgeted to be increased to 600 units at the end of April, 700 units at the end of May and 750 units at the end of June.

Each unit of the finished product requires 2 kg of raw materials which are purchased on credit in the month of production and cost £20 per kg payable one month after the date of purchase. At the beginning of March there will be 1,000 kg of raw materials in stock but these stock levels are to be decreased by 100 kg at the end of March and by 100 kg at the end of each month thereafter.

What are the payments to creditors in each of the months of April, May and June?

Solution

(a) Production budget

	March Units	April Units	May Units	June Units
Sales	4,000	4,200	4,400	4,600
Less: Opening stock (finished goods)	(500)	(500)	(600)	(700)
Add: Closing stock (finished goods)	500	600	700	750
Production quantity	4,000	4,300	4,500	4,650

Note that the closing finished goods stock at the end of each month is the opening stock at the start of the following month.

Once the amount of production is known then the raw materials purchases can be determined in quantities first of all. Start with the materials needed for the actual production but then take into consideration the fact that there is 1,000 kg of material at the start of March, but this stock level is to decrease by 100 kg per month thereafter.

(b) Materials purchases budget – kg

	March kgs	April kgs	May kgs	June kgs
Production × 2 kg	8,000	8,600	9,000	9,300
Less: Opening stock (raw materials)	(1,000)	(900)	(800)	(700)
Add: Closing stock (raw materials)	900	800	700	600
Purchases in kg	7,900	8,500	8,900	9,200

The materials purchases in each month are therefore the number of kg required at the price of £20 per kg.

Materials purchases budget – £

	March £	April £	May £	June £
Purchases in kg × £20	158,000	170,000	178,000	184,000

(c) Cash budget

Finally, the cash payments pattern is determined. In this case each month's purchases are paid for in the following month:

	April £	May £	June £	July £
Payments to creditors	158,000	170,000	178,000	184,000

5.5   Wages and salaries

Wages and salaries are normally paid in the month in which they are incurred and the only usual complication is that they may have to be calculated on a per unit basis based upon the production budget or there may be increases in the wage rate during the budget period.

You will generally start with the figures from the production budget calculated for materials as above (not the sales or purchases budget) and calculate the wages cost from that.

Example

The production budget for a company shows the following monthly production:

	April Units	May Units	June Units
Production	6,200	6,800	7,000

Each unit of production requires two labour hours and the wage rate is £7.00 per hour for April and May increasing to £7.40 per hour in June. Wages are paid in the month in which they are incurred.

What figures should appear for wages costs in the cash budget for April, May and June?

Solution

	April £	May £	June £
6,200 units × 2 × £7.00	86,800		
6,800 units × 2 × £7.00		95,200	
7,000 units × 2 × £7.40			103,600

5.6   Fixed overheads

Care should be taken with fixed overheads or expenses that are to appear in the cash budget. You will often be told that the monthly figure includes a certain amount which relates to depreciation. **Depreciation is not a cash flow and therefore this amount should be excluded from the cash budget.**

5.7 Overdraft interest

One of the purposes of a cash budget is to identify the cash balance at the end of each month and to determine whether an overdraft facility is required. If an overdraft is agreed with the bank and the facility is used then the bank will charge interest on the amount of the overdraft.

In practice the amount of the overdraft interest will be calculated on a daily basis. However for cash budgeting purposes the amount of overdraft interest will normally be calculated on the basis of the amount of the overdraft outstanding at the end of the previous month. This figure for interest will then be included in the following month's cash payments.

 Example

A business anticipates having an overdraft of £2,000 at the end of March. The budgeted cash receipts and payments (excluding overdraft interest) for the following three months are expected to be as follows:

	April £	May £	June £
Cash receipts	16,500	18,000	17,200
Cash payments	17,400	17,500	17,000

Overdraft interest is charged at 0.5% per month on the basis of the overdraft balance at the start of each month.

Prepare the completed cash budget including the amount of overdraft interest.

Solution

		April £	May £	June £
Cash receipts		16,500	18,000	17,200
Cash payments		(17,400)	(17,500)	(17,000)
Overdraft interest	(2,000 × 0.5%)	(10)		
	(2,910 × 0.5%)		(15)	
	(2,425 × 0.5%)			(12)
Net cash flow		(910)	485	188
Opening balance		(2,000)	(2,910)	(2,425)
Closing balance		(2,910)	(2,425)	(2,237)

Note that you can only calculate the overdraft interest month by month once you have calculated the opening cash balance of the relevant month.

6 Profit and loss adjustments

6.1 Adjusting profit and loss figures

It may be necessary to adjust profit and loss figures for balance sheet entries such as accruals and prepayments.

Definition

An accrual is an expense that has been incurred during the period but has not been paid for by the period end and has therefore not been entered in the ledger accounts.

A prepayment is a payment made during the period (and therefore debited to the expense account) for an expense that relates to a period after the year end.

It may also be necessary to use the balance sheet figures to work out how much cash has been received from debtors and creditors.

Example

The profit and loss account for L Boy's business for the quarter ended March is as follows:

	£	£
Sales		210,325
Less: Purchases		(32,657)
Gross profit		177,668
Less: Expenses		
Wages	50,100	
Rent of office	15,000	
Insurance of machinery	7,851	
Electricity	12,352	
Depreciation	8,687	
		(93,990)
Profit		83,678

Extracts from the balance sheet at 1 January and 31 March show the following:

	1 January	31 March
	£	£
Debtors	18,695	15,985
Creditors	965	1,054
Accruals – Electricity	550	450
Prepayments – Rent of office	1,200	1,350

Calculate the actual business cash receipts and cash payments for the quarter to 31 March

	Working	£
Sales receipts	18,695+210,325–15,985	213,035
Purchases	965+32,657–1,054	32,568
Wages	As per profit and loss	50,100
Rent of office	15,000–1,200+1,350	15,150
Insurance of machinery	As per profit and loss	7,851
Electricity	12,352+550–450	12,452
Depreciation	Non-cash item	0

Note: An opening prepayment has already been paid but the closing prepayment will be paid in this period (Rent). An opening accrual will be paid in the this period whereas the closing accrual will not (Electricity)

7 Worked example

7.1 Introduction

From the following information which relates to The Magic Lantern Company Limited, we are going to prepare a month by month cash budget for the second half of 20X5:

(a) A magic lantern sells for £40 and has a variable cost of £26 made up as follows:

Materials £20   Labour £4   Overhead £2

(b) Fixed costs amount to £6,000 per month and are paid on the 25th of each month.

(c)   Credit sales, in units:

May	June	July	Aug	Sept	Oct	Nov	Dec	Jan
1,000	1,200	1,400	1,600	1,800	2,000	2,200	2,600	2,400

(d)   Production quantities

The company produces goods one month before they are sold. The demand for the product fluctuates and the company therefore decides to adjust its stocks to cater for this as follows:

Month	Aug	Sept	Oct	Nov	Dec
Increase/(decrease) in stocks (units)	200	400	400	(200)	(200)

(e)   Cash sales, at a discount of 5%, are expected to average 100 units a month.

(f)   Customers are expected to settle their accounts within two months following the sale.

(g)   Suppliers of materials are paid two months after the materials are used in production.

(h)   Wages are paid in the same month as the magic lanterns are produced.

(i)   70% of the variable overhead is paid in the month of production and the remainder in the following month.

(j)   Corporation tax of £18,000 is to be paid in October.

(k)   A new delivery vehicle costing £8,000 was bought in June and is to be paid for in August. The old vehicle was sold for £600, the buyer undertaking to pay in July.

(l)   The company is expected to be £3,000 overdrawn at the bank at 30 June 20X5.

7.2   Approach to cash budget questions

The approach to a question like this is vital, especially under timed conditions. The key point to remember is that, unless you write a point down, the assessor will think that you do not know it. This means that the work should be done in the following order:

1   Read the question and be aware of what is in it.

2   Deal with the easy items first.

3   Only then attempt the more difficult items.

This approach will ensure that you do not omit points that you are able to deal with simply because you have run out of time.

7.3 Easy items

Having read the question and set out a proforma, return to the question and look for the easy items. Points (b), (j), (k) and (l) give information which can be copied straight from the question onto the answer.

Point (e) is also relatively easy to deal with, so we should also calculate the cash sales.

At this point, the answer is as follows

The Magic Lantern Company Limited
Cash budget for the six months to December 20X5

	July £	Aug £	Sept £	Oct £	Nov £	Dec £
Receipts						
Cash sales (W1)	3,800	3,800	3,800	3,800	3,800	3,800
Proceeds from sale of vehicle	600					
	July £	Aug £	Sept £	Oct £	Nov £	Dec £
Payments						
Fixed costs	6,000	6,000	6,000	6,000	6,000	6,000
Purchase of new vehicle		8,000				
Corporation tax				18,000		
Balance b/f	(3,000)					
Net cash flow						

Working 1

100 × £40 × 95% = £3,800

Note that the figures in the cash budget are cross-referenced to the appropriate workings.

This is not yet the finished article, but it is beginning to look like a cash budget and that provides encouragement to attempt the remainder of the question.

7.4 The final stage

Each question should be taken on its merits but, typically, production and hence associated cash flows will depend upon sales. So the next stage is usually to work out the credit sales figure and calculate when the cash is received.

(a) Calculate cash receipts from debtors

The cash received from credit sales is calculated as follows:

	May	June	July	Aug	Sept	Oct	Nov	Dec
Credit sales (units)	1,000	1,200	1,400	1,600	1,800	2,000	2,200	2,600
	£	£	£	£	£	£	£	£
Credit sales (£)	40,000	48,000	56,000	64,000	72,000	80,000	88,000	104,000
Cash received			40,000	48,000	56,000	64,000	72,000	80,000

Having calculated the cash received, write the information on the cash budget.

(b) Calculate the production budget

Now that sales are known (not forgetting the cash sales) we can work out our production.

	April	May	June	July	Aug	Sept	Oct	Nov	Dec	Jan
Credit sales (units)	–	1,000	1,200	1,400	1,600	1,800	2,000	2,200	2,600	2,400
Cash sales (units)	–	100	100	100	100	100	100	100	100	100
Total sales (units)	–	1,100	1,300	1,500	1,700	1,900	2,100	2,300	2,700	2,500
Production for sales (one month before) (units)	1,100	1,300	1,500	1,700	1,900	2,100	2,300	2,700	2,500	–
Stock increase/ (decrease) (units)	–	–	–	–	200	400	400	(200)	(200)	–
Total production (units)	1,100	1,300	1,500	1,700	2,100	2,500	2,700	2,500	2,300	–

(c) Calculate the materials purchases budget

Now that production is known, we can work out the material cost and when that cost is paid.

	April	May	June	July	Aug	Sept	Oct	Nov	Dec
Production (units)	1,100	1,300	1,500	1,700	2,100	2,500	2,700	2,500	2,300
	£	£	£	£	£	£	£	£	£
Material cost of production (£20 per unit)	22,000	26,000	30,000	34,000	42,000	50,000	54,000	50,000	46,000

(d) Cash payments to supplier's budget

	April	May	June	July	Aug	Sept	Oct	Nov	Dec
Two month delay (units)	–	–	22,000	26,000	30,000	34,000	42,000	50,000	54,000

This information should now be written onto the cash budget.

(e) Calculate the wages and variable overhead

Start with the production budget and work out wages and overheads from that.

	June	July	Aug	Sept	Oct	Nov	Dec
Units produced	1,500	1,700	2,100	2,500	2,700	2,500	2,300
	£	£	£	£	£	£	£
Wages paid (£4 per unit)	6,000	6,800	8,400	10,000	10,800	10,000	9,200
Variable overhead (£2 per unit)	3,000	3,400	4,200	5,000	5,400	5,000	4,600
Cash paid							
70% in month	2,100	2,380	2,940	3,500	3,780	3,500	3,220
30% next month	–	900	1,020	1,260	1,500	1,620	1,500
Total variable overhead paid		3,280	3,960	4,760	5,280	5,120	4,720

Note that wages are paid in the month of production but in this question 70% of overheads are paid in the month of production and 30% are paid in the month following production.

7.5 Complete solution

The Magic Lantern Company Limited
Cash budget for the six months to December 20X5

	July £	Aug £	Sept £	Oct £	Nov £	Dec £
Receipts						
Cash from debtors	40,000	48,000	56,000	64,000	72,000	80,000
Cash sales (W1)	3,800	3,800	3,800	3,800	3,800	3,800
Proceeds from sale of vehicle	600					
	44,400	51,800	59,800	67,800	75,800	83,800

	July £	Aug £	Sept £	Oct £	Nov £	Dec £
Payments						
Fixed costs	6,000	6,000	6,000	6,000	6,000	6,000
Payments to creditors	26,000	30,000	34,000	42,000	50,000	54,000
Wages	6,800	8,400	10,000	10,800	10,000	9,200
Variable overhead	3,280	3,960	4,760	5,280	5,120	4,720
Corporation tax				18,000		
Purchase of new vehicle		8,000				
	42,080	56,360	54,760	82,080	71,120	73,920
Summary						
Balance b/f	(3,000)	(680)	(5,240)	(200)	(14,480)	(9,800)
Net cash flow	2,320	(4,560)	5,040	(14,280)	4,680	9,880
Balance c/f	(680)	(5,240)	(200)	(14,480)	(9,800)	80

This shows that until December the company will have an overdraft, which will rise as high as £14,480 in October.

 Activity 4

Data

Kirkton Jeans Limited started in business on 1 November 20X4 with share capital of £200,000. It received £100,000 in enterprise grants from a Regional Enterprise Company and has negotiated a £325,000 overdraft facility from a local bank.

The company is a fashion manufacturer specialising in the manufacture of denim jeans for the domestic market. At the commencement of business, the company bought cutting and sewing machinery costing £130,000 and fixtures and fittings of £11,000.

Kirkton Jeans will sell a small range of denim jeans, each with a similar cost structure and sold at a similar price:

	£	£
Selling price		15.00
Costs		
Direct labour	6.50	
Direct material	3.25	
Variable overheads	1.50	
	——	11.25
Contribution		3.75

Fixed overheads are property expenses of £240,000 per annum, paid monthly in advance, and energy costs of £115,200 per annum, paid quarterly in arrears in February, May, August and November. Other fixed costs are estimated at £15,000 per month, to be paid monthly. Forecast sales in units are as follows:

Nov	Dec	Jan
Nil	20,000	24,000

The planned production profile is as follows:

Nov	Dec	Jan
24,000	24,000	22,000

50% of sales are for cash. The remainder are credit sales. Industry experience and market research suggests that all credit sales will be paid in the month following sale (i.e. 'net monthly').

Material purchases are paid for in the month incurred. Labour costs and variable overheads are also paid for in the month in which they are incurred.

The bank charges interest on overdrafts at the rate of 1% per month, calculated on the closing balance at the end of the month. Interest is then paid on the first banking day of the following month.

Task

Using the proforma cash flow budget supplied, prepare a month-by-month cash flow for Kirkton Jeans Limited.

Kirkton Jeans Limited

	Nov £	Dec £	Jan £
RECEIPTS			
Cash sales	0	150,000	360,000
Cash from debtors	0	0	150,000
Share capital	200,000	0	0
Enterprise grants	100,000	0	0
Total receipts	300,000	150,000	510,000
PAYMENTS			
Direct labour	156 000	156 000	143 000
Material purchase	78 000	78 000	71 500
Variable overheads	36 000	36 000	33 000
Property costs	20,000	20,000	20,000
Energy costs	22 000	0	0
Other fixed costs	15 000	15 000	15 000
Capital costs	141 000	0	0
Interest			
Total payments	446 000	305 000	182 500
Net cash flow	(146 000)		
Opening bank balance	325 000	(146 000)	
Closing bank balance	(146 000)		

Activity 5

Data

Wilson Limited produces bicycle saddles. By increasing exports, it plans to increase production and sales during the first half of next year. The actual figures for November and December were as follows.

Month (20X6)	Production (units)	Sales (units)
November	7,000	7,000
December	8,000	8,000

The plans for the next six months are shown below.

Month (20X7)	Production (units)	Sales (units)
January	10,000	8,000
February	12,000	10,000
March	12,000	12,000

- The selling price is £20.50 per unit

- Raw material costs £4 per unit.

- Wages and other variable costs are £8 per unit.

- Other fixed costs are £1,800 per month including £200 of depreciation.

- 20% of sales are for cash, the remainder being credit sales which are paid for two months after the sale.

- Material purchases are paid one month after delivery and are held in stock for one month before entering production.

- Wages and variable and fixed costs are paid in the month of production.

- A new machine costing £300,000 is to be purchased in February to cope with the planned expansion of demand. 20% of payment is to be made on 1 February and the remainder retained until the machine is operational (expected 1 July 20X7).

- An advertising campaign is also to be launched, involving payments of £20,000 in each of February and May.

- Corporation tax of £56,000 is due to be paid on 30 March 20X7.

- The company is financed by share capital of 1 million £1 shares and a debenture of £0.5 million paying semi-annual interest of 3.5% on 30 March and 31 September.

- The directors plan to pay a dividend of £0.10 per share in February.

- An overdraft of £0.5 million has been agreed with Wilson Limited's bankers.

- The current overdraft interest rate is 7.2% per annum on the prior month closing balance.

- Interest is received on cash balances at 6.0% per annum on the prior month closing balance.

- On 1 January the firm expects to have £185,000 in the bank.

Task

Complete the cash budget provided below.

Wilson Limited – Cash budget 20X7

	Jan £	Feb £	Mar £
RECEIPTS			
Cash sales			
Cash from debtors			
Interest received			
Total receipts			
PAYMENTS			
Payment to creditors for materials			
Variable costs			
Fixed costs			
Advertising			
Capital expenditure			
Corporation tax			
Dividends			
Interest on overdraft			
Interest on long-term loan			
Total payments			
Net cash flow			
Opening bank balance			
Closing bank balance			

8 Summary

When the estimated cash receipts and payments are brought together in a cash budget then the estimated net cash position at the end of each month can be determined and management can take action to deal with this net cash position in the most appropriate manner.

The preparation of a cash budget requires a logical approach to determining the more difficult cash flows such as cash from credit sales or cash paid to creditors. Make sure that you do put in all of the easy figures as well as spending your time on the more complicated calculations.

 Test your knowledge

Having completed Chapter 2 you should now be able to attempt:

Practice Activities 6 to 13

Answers to chapter activities

Activity 1

Regular revenue receipt – F

Exceptional payment – H

Capital payment – B

Drawings – C

Annual disbursement – I

Activity 2

	June £	July £	Aug £
Sales units	3,000	2,900	3,190
Selling price per unit	45	48	48
Sales	135,000	139,200	153,120
Of which are:			
Cash	22,500	24,000	24,000
Credit	112,500	115,200	129,120
The cash receipts from the debtors will be:			
60% in month of sale less 2% discount	66,150	67,738	75,923
40% in subsequent month	41,400	45,000	46,080
Giving:			
Total cash receipts	130,050	136,738	146,003

Activity 3

	May £	June £	July £	Aug £
Purchases	100,000	110,000	120,000	130,000
Payments to creditors				
Cash (30%)	30,000	33,000	36,000	39,000
In the month of purchase	33,250	36,575	39,900	43,225
One month after purchase		21,000	23,100	25,200
Two months after purchase			14,000	15,400
Cash payments			113,000	122,825

Activity 4

	Nov £	Dec £	Jan £
RECEIPTS			
Cash sales – 50% of sales × £15	–	150,000	180,000
Cash from debtors – remainder of sales 1 month later	–	–	150,000
Share capital	200,000	–	–
Enterprise grants	100,000	–	–
Total receipts	300,000	150,000	330,000
PAYMENTS			
Direct labour – production × £6.50	156,000	156,000	143,000
Material purchase – production × £3.25	78,000	78,000	71,500
Variable overheads – production × £1.50	36,000	36,000	33,000
Property costs – 240,000/12	20,000	20,000	20,000
Energy costs – 115,200/3 but in arrears	–	–	–
Other fixed costs	15,000	15,000	15,000
Capital costs	141,000	–	–
Interest – 1% of closing balance of prior month	–	1,460	3,025
Total payments	446,000	306,460	285,525
Net cash flow	(146,000)	(156,460)	44,475
Opening bank balance	0	(146,000)	(32,460)
Closing bank balance	(146,000)	(302,460)	(346,935)

Activity 5

Wilson Limited: cash budget 20X7

	Jan £	Feb £	Mar £
RECEIPTS			
Cash sales sales × £20.50 × 20%	32,800	41,000	49,200
Cash from debtors sales × £20.50 × 80%	114,800	131,200	131,200
Interest received 185,000 × (6%/12)	925	1,060	730
Total receipts	148,525	173,260	181,130
PAYMENTS			
Payment to creditors for materials* Production × £4	40,000	48,000	48,000
Variable costs Production × £8	80,000	96,000	96,000
Fixed costs £1,800 - £200	1,600	1,600	1,600
Advertising	–	20,000	–
Capital expenditure	–	60,000	–
Corporation tax	–	–	56,000
Dividends £0.10 × 1,000,000 shares	–	100,000	–
Interest on overdraft	–	–	–
Interest on long-term loan £500,000 × 3.5%	–	–	17,500
Total payments	121,600	239,200	219,100
Net cash flow	26,925	(65,940)	(37,970)
Opening bank balance	185,000	211,925	145,985
Closing bank balance	211,925	145,985	108,015

* Materials for January will be purchased in December and then paid for in January

Forecasting and monitoring cash flows

Introduction

This chapter begins with consideration of methods that can be used to forecast cash payments and cash receipts. One of the most common of these methods is time series analysis which can be used to try to forecast as accurately as possible sales in future periods. Cash flow forecasts might also be affected by changes in quantities of sales or production and by inflation of costs and prices.

Once a cash flow forecast has been prepared then it has a variety of uses to management. By changing individual assumptions within the forecast it is possible to see what effect this might have on the eventual cash balance. Finally this chapter considers how cash flows will be monitored and how the cash flow forecast will be compared to the actual cash flows and the importance of this area for management.

KNOWLEDGE
Explain techniques that can be used for estimating future trends: moving averages; allowance for inflation (3.5)

SKILLS
Ensure forecasts of future cash payments and receipts agree with known income and expenditure trends (1.2)
Monitor cash receipts and payments against budgeted cash flow (2.1)
Identify significant deviations from the cash budget and take corrective action within organisational policies (2.2)
Take account of trends in the economic and financial environment in managing cash balances (3.2)

CONTENTS

1   Information for cash budgets

2   Time series

3   Time series analysis

4   Percentage change

5   Index numbers

6   Sensitivity to cash budget elements

7   Monitoring cash flow

1 Information for cash budgets

1.1 Introduction

In the previous chapter we have seen how much information is required in order to produce a cash budget so you need to know where the information comes from.

1.2 Sales information

The starting point for information for the cash budget will normally be sales quantities and prices as this will be the basis for the production budget and expenses figures. The sales information will normally be provided by the **sales or marketing director or manager**. Both the quantity of sales and the price that will be charged is vital for the cash budget and we will look at methods of estimating future sales later in the chapter.

1.3 Production information

Details such as the amount of production, the levels of closing stocks and the labour hours to be worked should all be available from the **production manager or director**. The production manager may also have information about variable and fixed expenses of the factory but equally that information may come from the accountant.

The production manager or director may also be able to provide information about any planned capital expenditure or any planned sales of fixed assets.

1.4 Accounting information

Some further information required may come from the **accounts department** in the form of materials prices, labour hour rates, variable and fixed costs, details of sales of fixed assets. The accounts department should also have the information required to determine the payment pattern of debtors and creditors.

1.5 Forecast information

All of this information required for the cash budget has to be forecast. This will start with forecasts of **sales quantities** which could be done using time series analysis. The **sales price** must also be forecast and this may be done by considering inflation rates.

Once the sales figures have been forecast the **production expenses** must be estimated which will include forecasts of materials prices, wage rates and expense items.

2 Time series

2.1 Introduction

The sales director may know that sales are changing but may not be able to quantify the changes without undertaking some basic analysis. A method of finding the underlying trend is to use time series analysis which enables a general linear trend to be isolated from a fluctuating pattern of changing values.

 Definition

A time series is a set of values for some variable (e.g. monthly sales) which varies with time. The set of observations will be taken at specific times, usually at regular intervals.

Examples of figures which can be plotted as a time series are:

(a) monthly rainfall in London

(b) daily closing price of a share on the Stock Exchange

(c) weekly sales in a department store.

2.2 Time series graph

The graph below shows the sales volume for a year in a business. In such a graph, each point is joined by a straight line – hence the typically 'jagged' appearance. For this graph to be useful for predicting cash flows the 'trend' or general movement of the data needs to be known – is it increasing, decrease or staying static?

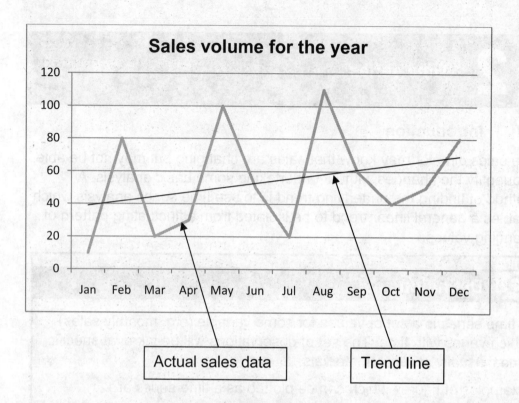

Actual sales data

Trend line

2.3 Characteristic movements

Analysis of time series has revealed certain characteristic movements or variations. These movements are the components of the time series. Analysis of these components is essential for forecasting purposes.

The four main types of components are:

*   basic trends or long-term movements
*   cyclical movements
*   seasonal movements
*   residual or random movements.

2.4 Basic trend

The basic trend refers to the **general direction** in which the graph of a time series goes over a long interval of time. This movement can be represented on the graph by a trend curve or line.

For the graph above you can see that the basic trend is for sales to be increasing over the year.

2.5 Cyclical variations

Cyclical variations refer to **long-term oscillations** or swings about the trend line or curve. These cycles may or may not be periodic; i.e. they do **not necessarily follow exactly similar patterns** after equal intervals of time. In business and economic situations, movements are said to be cyclical if they recur after time intervals of **more than one year**. A good example is the trade cycle, representing intervals of prosperity, recession, depression and recovery.

For cyclical variations to be apparent, data must be available over very long periods of time since the periods of oscillation are so long. This is impractical for cash flows and, for that reason, the **calculation of cyclical variations is ignored in this chapter** although you must, of course, realise that they exist.

2.6 Seasonal variations

Seasonal fluctuations are the **identical, or almost identical, patterns** which a time series follows during corresponding intervals of successive periods. Such movements are due to recurring events, such as the sudden increase in department store sales before Christmas. Although, in general, seasonal movements refer to a period of one year, this is not always the case and **periods of hours, days, weeks, months**, etc may also be considered, depending on the type of data available.

2.7 Random variations

Random variations are the **sporadic motions** of time series due to chance events such as **floods, strikes, elections** etc.

By their very nature they are **unpredictable** and therefore cannot play a large part in any forecasting, but it is possible to isolate the random variations by calculating all other types of variation and removing them from the time series data. It is important to extract any significant random variations from the data before using them for forecasting.

3 Time series analysis

3.1 Analysis of a time series

The analysis of a time series consists of:

Step 1 Breaking the series down into trend and seasonal variations

Step 2 Projecting the trend into the future.

Step 3 Adding together the projected trend and seasonal variation to arrive at one forecast figure.

3.2 Isolating the trend

There are many methods of analysing time series; some sophisticated, others simple. The method covered in this chapter is the best known and most commonly used, though not necessarily the most sophisticated.

You may have noticed earlier that a trend curve was drawn in on the time series graph. Indeed one way of isolating the trend, admittedly not very scientific, is **simply to draw it in freehand on the graph**.

This is not usually good enough for most purposes and we will use the method of **moving averages** in order to isolate the trend figures.

3.3 Moving averages

By using moving averages, the **variations in a time series can be eliminated leaving a 'smoothed' set of figures** which is taken as the trend. It is important that the correct cycle is chosen for the moving average otherwise the result will not be as good as it should be. For instance, if there are seasonal variations present in a time series and the pattern is repeated every fourth period, then moving averages with a cycle of 4 should be used for the best results.

In the assessment the moving average will be an odd-point moving average so you will be doing either a 3-point or 5-point moving average.

 Example

The following data will be used to demonstrate the various techniques in the subsequent paragraphs. The figures shown are the quarterly sales figures.

The underlying trend is estimated using moving averages.

(a) Month	(b) Value	(c) 3 month moving total	(d) Trend (T) (c)/3
Jan	74		
Feb	100	268 (W1)	90
Mar	94	278 (W2)	93
Apr	84	284	95
May	106	290	97
Jun	100	290	97
Jul	88	303	101
Aug	115	308	103
Sept	105	312	104
Oct	92	314	105
Nov	117	318	106
Dec	109		

Positioning of figures in column (c) and (d) should be noted.

- Points on column (c)

    (W1) 268 is the total of the first three months (i.e.74 + 100 + 94).
    (W2) 321 is the total of months 2 to 4 (i.e. 100 + 94 + 84)

- Point on column (e)

    The trend can now be found, by taking the three-month moving total and dividing by 3 (e.g. 268 / 3 = 90 rounded). This average figure is the average of months 1, 2 and 3 and is taken to represent month 2's trend figure

Activity 1

The following represents quarterly output of a product:

Jan	Feb	Mar	Apr	May	Jun	Jul	Aug	Sept
12	25	18	15	30	21	19	32	25

What are the trend figures that would be obtained by a 3-month moving average?

Month	Value	3-month moving total	Trend
Jan	12		
Feb	25		
Mar	18		
Apr	15		
May	30		
Jun	21		
Jul	19		
Aug	32		
Sept	25		

Activity 2

Seasonal variations or fluctuations may affect many companies' cash flows.

The table below provides details of Masham plc's monthly cash flow.

Calculate the three-month moving average of Masham's cash flow (to the nearest thousand) in the spaces provided below.

Month	Sales value (000s)	3 month moving total	Trend
June	770		
July	750		
August	910		
September	905		
October	925		
November	870		
December	990		

3.4 Calculating the variation

Once the trend is identified it is then possible to calculate the variation to be able to predict the next set of data.

 Example

A company is preparing its forecast sales for the first quarter of next year. Identify the sales volume trend from this year's data (below) using a 3-month moving average and calculate the monthly sales trend and variation. Use this information to predict January, February and March's sales volume for next year.

Solution

Month	Sales volume (a)	3 Month Trend (b)	Monthly variation = a – b
Jan	4,000		
Feb	8,680	5,980	2,700
Mar	5,260	6,160	–900
Apr	4,540	6,340	–1,800
May	9,220	6,520	2,700
Jun	5,800	6,700	–900
Jul	5,080	6,880	–1,800
Aug	9,760	7,060	2,700
Sept	6,340	7,240	–900
Oct	5,620	7,420	–1,800
Nov	10,300	7,600	2,700
Dec	6,880		

The monthly sales volume trend is 180 units as this is the increase in the trend each month. The monthly variation is the actual sales volume less the trend and there is also a pattern to the variation.

Month	Forecast sales trend	Variation	Forecast sale volume
Jan	7,780	–1,800	5,980
Feb	7,960	2,700	10,660
Mar	8,140	–900	7,240

The variation is 'from the trend' therefore a negative variation means that the actual sales volume will be less than the trend and the positive variation will be higher than the trend

Activity 3

A company is preparing its forecast sales for the first quarter of next year. Identify the sales volume trend from this year's data (below) using a 3-month moving average and calculate the percentage change in monthly sales and the variation. Use this information to predict March, April and May's sales volume for next year.

Month	Sales volume	3 Month Trend	Monthly variation
Jan	4,600		
Feb	5,300	5000	300
Mar	5,100	5150	– 50
Apr	5,050	5300	– 250
May	5,750	5450	300
Jun	5,550	5600	– 50
Jul	5,500	5750	– 250
Aug	6,200	5900	300
Sept	6,000	6050	– 50
Oct	5,950	6200	– 250
Nov	6,650	6350	300
Dec	6,450	6500	

The monthly sales volume trend is

Month	Forecast sales trend	Variation	Forecast sale volume
Mar	6950	– 50	6900
Apr	7100	– 250	6850
May	7250	+ 300	7550

3.5 Disadvantages of moving averages

- Values at the beginning and end of the series are lost; therefore, the moving averages do not cover the complete period.

- The moving averages may generate cycles or other movements that were not present in the original data.

- The averages are strongly affected by extreme values. To overcome this, a weighted moving average is sometimes used, giving the largest weights to central items and small weights to extreme values.

4 Percentage change

4.1 Introduction

In arriving at expected sales, purchases and other cost figures, department heads may use percentage changes or inflation. It is also possible to use indexes to predict future trends

4.2 Percentage changes – quantity

In some situations, it may be quite easy to predict future sales. From past experience and knowledge of the market, a sales director may predict sales quantities to rise by 1% each month.

So, for example, if sales are 100,000 units at £1 each (i.e. £100,000 in January), he could predict:

February	$(100{,}000 \times 1.01)$	=	101,000 units
March	$(100{,}000 \times 1.01^2)$ (i.e. $100 \times 1.01 \times 1.01$)	=	102,010 units
April etc	$(100{,}000 \times 1.01^3)$	=	103,030 units

4.3 Percentage changes – price

Alternatively, the only rise in sales may be due to **inflation**, say of 3% per month, which means the price rises. So, if January sales are £100,000, then:

February sales will be	$(£100{,}000 \times 1.03)$	=	£103,000
March sales will be	$(£103{,}000 \times 1.03)$	=	£106,090 etc

4.4 Quantity and price changes

Sales may be both rising by 1% in volume terms and increasing in value by 3% due to inflation each month. In which case, when January sales are 100,000 units × £1 = £100,000:

February sales will be	$(100{,}000 \times 1.01)$ units × $(£1 \times 1.03)$	=	£104,030
March sales will be	$(100{,}000 \times 1.01^2)$ units × $(£1 \times 1.03^2)$	=	£108,222 etc

5 Index numbers

5.1 Introduction

Definition

An **index number** is a means of explaining changes over time in economic variables such as prices, wages, output, etc.

It shows how these items **change with time** and can be divided into three types:

(a) **price index numbers**, which measure changes in prices

(b) **quantity index numbers**, which measure changes in quantity

(c) **value index numbers**, which measure changes in the value of services or activities of goods.

5.2 Using an index

An index is a useful method of comparing figures over time by simplifying them to a single index figure that can be compared to a base year which is given an index of 100. The index then shows the change in the figures each year comparison to that base year.

Example

Given below are the production cost figures for a business for the last eight years:

Year	Cost £000
20X0	138
20X1	149
20X2	158
20X3	130
20X4	136
20X5	150
20X6	154
20X7	162

You are to calculate an index for these costs using 20X0 as the base year.

Solution

The formula for calculation of each year's index is:

$$\frac{\text{Current year costs}}{\text{Base year costs}} \times 100$$

We can now calculate the index for each year:

Year	Cost £000	Calculation	Index
20X0	138	138/138 × 100	100.0
20X1	149	149/138 × 100	108.0
20X2	158	158/138 × 100	114.5
20X3	130	130/138 × 100	94.2
20X4	136	136/138 × 100	98.6
20X5	150	150/138 × 100	108.7
20X6	154	154/138 × 100	111.6
20X7	162	162/138 × 100	117.4

The indices that are above 100 show that the costs have increased over the 20X0 costs in that year. The indices that are below 100 show that the costs are lower in that year than in 20X0.

We can now see clearly from the index figures that costs rose for two years then fell below 20X0 levels for two years before continuing to rise substantially.

5.3   Price index numbers

If the price of one item is recorded at different times, then an index number can be constructed to show **changes in price.**

The index number or price relative is:

$$\frac{\text{Current price of item}}{\text{Base price of item}} \times 100$$

Example

Year	Price of car service
20X0	£36.50
20X1	£39.20
20X2	£44.70
20X3	£51.40
20X4	£52.50

Taking 20X1 as the base year calculate an index for these prices.

Solution

The index for 20X0 is:

$$\frac{36.50}{39.20} \times 100 = 93.1$$

Similarly, for 20X2:

$$\frac{44.70}{39.20} \times 100 = 114.0$$

And if the other years' index numbers are calculated:

20X3 $\dfrac{51.40}{39.20} \times 100 = 131.1$

20X4 $\dfrac{52.50}{39.20} \times 100 = 133.9$

5.4   Using the index

The figures obtained above are index numbers. All the figures are calculated as percentages of the figure for 20X1 and so they show percentage changes from 20X1 (e.g. the price for 20X3 is 31.1% higher than that in 20X1).

However, you cannot say the percentage rise from 20X3 to 20X4 is:

133.9 – 131.1 = 2.8%

It is in fact:

$$\frac{52.50}{51.40} \times 100 = 102.1$$

so a 2.1% increase has occurred. We could use the appropriate index numbers to find this increase from 20X3 to 20X4:

$$\frac{133.9}{131.1} \times 100 = 102.1 \text{ (as before)}$$

5.5 Quantity index

The idea of an index is not limited to prices. Suppose the number of cars serviced at a garage is known. Then, an index with base year 20X1 is calculated as:

Year	Number of cars	Index number	
20X0	2,138	$\frac{2,138}{2,210} \times 100 =$	96.7
20X1	2.210		100.0
20X2	3,256	$\frac{2,356}{2,210} \times 100 =$	106.6
20X3	2,199	$\frac{2,199}{2,210} \times 100 =$	99.5
20X4	2,056	$\frac{2,056}{2,210} \times 100 =$	93.0

This is called a **quantity index.**

Activity 4

A company is preparing its forecast sales for next year 20Y2. Calculate the index for each month based on 20Y1 figures with January as the base month. Then predict how the sales will change over 20Y2.

Sales units for 20Y1

Month	Sales (units)	Calculation	Index
January	50,000	50/ 50 x 100	100
February	55,000	55/ 50 x 100	110
March	52,000	52/ 50 x 100	104
April	60,000	60 / 50 x 100	120
May	64,000	64 / 50 x 100	128
June	48,000	48 / 50 x 100	96
July	46,000	46 / 50 x 100	92
August	49,000	49 / 50 x 100	98
September	51,000	51 / 50 x 100	102
October	52,000	52 / 50 x 100	104
November	55,000	55 / 50 x 100	110
December	53,000	53 / 50 x 100	106

Forecast for 20Y2

Month	Index	Calculation	Forecast sale volume
January	100	100/ 100 x 52	52,000
February	110	110 / 100 x 52	57200
March	104	104 / 100 x 52	54080
April	120	120 / 100 x 52	62400
May	128	128 / 100 x 52	66560
June	96	96 / 100 x 52	49920
July	92	92 / 100 x 52	47840
August	98	98 / 100 x 52	50960
September	102	102 / 100 x 52	53040
October	104	106 / 100 x 52	54080
November	110	110 / 100 x 52	57200
December	106	106 / 100 x 52	55120

5.6 Retail Prices Index (RPI)

One of the most commonly used indices is the Retail Prices Index. This is an index compiled by the Department of Employment and published monthly in the Department of Employment Gazette and Monthly Digest of Statistics.

 Definition

The **general index of retail prices** measures the percentage changes month by month in the average level of prices of commodities and services purchased by the great majority of households in the UK, including practically all wage earners and most small and medium salary earners.

The RPI is often used as a measure of general inflation in the country.

5.7 Industry sector average index

An industry sector average is simply an average figure for a particular variable that is measured for a particular sector of industry for a particular period.

For example the average may be calculated for prices in retail male clothing for the year ended 31 December 19X8.

There are clearly millions of possible industry averages that can be calculated. The index above could be divided into several averages by distinguishing between male children's clothing and male adult clothing.

An industry sector average index is an index that compares the average over a period of time. Thus the industry average of prices of men's clothing could be turned into an index using the techniques we have already studied.

 Example

The hourly wage for agricultural workers in Wiltshire for 20X4 was found by sending a questionnaire to a sample of 2,000 farms asking for the number of agricultural workers employed and their average hourly wage for each farm. The figures were collected and an average produced for all 2,000 farms.

The results for 20X4 showed that the average hourly wage was £8.75.

The results for the previous three years were:

Year	Average hourly wage £
20X1	7.50
20X2	8.10
20X3	8.50

Calculate the average hourly wage index using 20X1 as the base year.

Solution

Year	Average hourly wage £		Index
20X1	7.50	(7.50/7.50) × 100	100.0
20X2	8.10	(8.10/7.50) × 100	108.0
20X3	8.50	(8.50/7.50) × 100	113.3
20X4	8.75	(8.75/7.50) × 100	116.7

 Activity 5

A company uses an industry wage rate index to forecast monthly wage costs. Employees receive a pay rise in September each year. The current monthly cost is £7,800 was calculated when the wage index was 134. The forecast wage rate index for the next three months is:

August   152

September   162

October   168

What will the wage cost be for September, to the nearest £?

A   £6,452

B   £6,876

C   £9,430

D   £8,848

5.8 Deflating a series using the Retail Prices Index (RPI)

If a series of figures is concerned with **sums of money and recorded through time** then it will be affected by **inflation** and so changes can be misleading. One often hears comments such as '£1.50 for a pint of beer! It was only 2s 4d when I was a boy'. The important factor is, how long did someone have to work to earn the 2s 4d to buy the original pint and how long does he now have to work to buy the current pint?

To overcome this, **'real prices' are found by deflating the original series**. This is effectively changing the money values to values at one point in time, the base time, and so making the figures directly comparable.

⋮◯⋮ Example

Consider the following table of average weekly pay and the RPI, by year:

Year	Average weekly wage £	RPI
20X5	69.50	91.0
20X6	78.40	98.6
20X7	90.10	111.8
20X8	108.60	131.9
20X9	120.30	145.9

Solution

The 'real' value of earnings in relation to 20X5 would be calculated as:

$$\text{Average wage for year} \times \frac{\text{RPI for base year}}{\text{RPI for current year}}$$

This gives for 20X6, a deflated figure of:

$$£78.40 \times \frac{91.0}{98.6} = £72.36$$

Similarly, for 20X7 the deflated figure is:

$$£90.10 \times \frac{91.0}{111.8} \times £73.34$$

For 20X8 the deflated figure is:

$$£108.60 \times \frac{91.0}{131.9} = £74.92$$

And for 20X9 the deflated figure is:

$$£120.30 \times \frac{91.0}{145.9} = £75.03$$

Bringing this information together in one table, gives:

Year	Average weekly wage £	RPI	'Real' weekly wage (20X5) £
20X5	69.50	91.0	69.50
20X6	78.40	98.6	72.36
20X7	90.10	111.8	73.34
20X8	108.60	131.9	74.92
20X9	120.30	145.9	75.03

Looking at the change from 20X5 to 20X9 shows that the purchasing power of average wages has risen by:

$$\frac{75.03 - 69.50}{369.50} \times 100$$

$$= \frac{5.53}{69.50} \times 100 = 7.96\%$$

 Activity 6

Energy supplies

Given below is the sales revenue of a business from 20X1 to 20X5 and the average RPI for each year.

Year	Sales £	RPI
20X1	486,000	111.8
20X2	521,000	131.9
20X3	562,000	145.9
20X4	604,000	150.3
20X5	683,000	156.3

Required

Deflate the sales revenue using the RPI to show all revenue in terms of 20X1 prices.

Year	Sales revenue	Calculation	Deflated sales revenue
	£	£	£
20X1	486,000		
20X2	521,000		
20X3	562,000		
20X4	604,000		
20X5	683,000		

6 Sensitivity of the cash budget elements

6.1 Introduction

In many cases managers may need to consider how the bank position will alter if there is a change in any of the receipt or expenditure items. What may seem a healthy positive cash position could change with a 1% increase in wages or a 2% fall in sales. It is therefore advisable to assess the sensitivity of the balance to such changes.

Example

Consider the following cash flow.

	January £	February £	March £
Receipts			
Sales	10,000	20,000	15,000
Payments			
Creditors	10,000	10,000	20,000
Wages	2,000	3,000	2,000
Sundry	500	500	500
	12,500	13,500	22,500
Net cash flow	(2,500)	6,500	(7,500)
Balance b/f	4,000	1,500	8,000
Balance c/f	1,500	8,000	500

What would be the net cash position each month if:

(i) wages increased by 5%?

(ii) wages increased by 8%?

Solution

(i) If wages increase by 5% you can see that the wage expense will become:

	£	£	£
Wages	2,100	3,150	2,100

and the bank balance changes to:

	£	£	£
Net cash flow	(2,600)	6,350	(7,600)
Balance b/f	4,000	1,400	7,750
Balance c/f	1,400	7,750	150

Thus, although wages have increased, the bank balance is still positive and corrective measures are not required.

(ii) If, however, an 8% wage increase were agreed, then wages would become:

	£	£	£
Wages	2,160	3,240	2,160
causing:			
Net cash flow	(2,660)	6,260	(7,660)
Balance b/f	4,000	1,340	7,600
Balance c/f	1,340	7,600	(60)

i.e. the bank balance would become overdrawn.

6.2 Changes in payment patterns

The cash flows that appear in the cash budget are heavily dependent upon the payment patterns of debtors or the timescale on which the business pays its creditors. In some cases managers may need information about the effect that a change in those payment patterns would have on the net cash position.

 Example

A business is producing its cash budget for the next three months. Credit sales in February and March were £50,000 and £58,000. Credit sales are forecast as £60,000, £70,000 and £50,000 respectively for each of the months of April, May and June. Credit customers are currently offered one month's credit and they all pay in the month after the sale.

Cash outflows in each month are estimated to be:

April	May	June
£48,000	£57,000	£60,000

At the end of March there is an overdraft of £10,000.

What would be the effect on the net cash position at the end of each month if credit customers took two months' credit?

Solution

Current policy cash budget (one month credit)

	April £	May £	June £
Receipts from debtors (previous months sales)	58,000	60,000	70,000
Cash outflows	(48,000)	(57,000)	(60,000)
Net cash flow	10,000	3,000	10,000
Cash balance b/f	(10,000)	–	3,000
Cash balance c/f	–	3,000	13,000

New policy cash budget (two months credit)

	April £	May £	June £
Receipts from debtors (sales from two months ago)	50,000	58,000	60,000
Cash outflows	(48,000)	(57,000)	(60,000)
Net cash flow	2,000	1,000	–
Cash balance b/f	(10,000)	(8,000)	(7,000)
Cash balance c/f	(8,000)	(7,000)	(7,000)

The effect of debtors paying two months after the sale rather than one month has been to reduce a positive cash balance to an overdraft balance at the end of each month.

Activity 7

	April £	May £	June £
Sales	2,600	3,100	1,600
Creditors	1,300	1,550	700
Wages	1,000	1,000	1,000
Power	200	200	200
	2,500	2,750	1,900
Balance b/f	100	200	550
Net cash flow	100	350	(300)
Balance c/f	200	550	250

In the above cash flow, how sensitive is the bank balance at the end of June to a 1% increase and a 2% decrease in sales?

1% increase

	April £	May £	June £
Sales			
Increase/(decrease) New net cash flow			
Balance b/f	100		
Balance c/f			

2% decrease

	April £	May £	June £
Sales			
Increase/(decrease) New net cash flow			
Balance b/f	100		
Balance c/f			

6.3 Discount to credit customers

A further way in which the payment pattern of debtors can be altered is by the offering of a cash or settlement discount for earlier payment of outstanding debts. This will mean that less cash will be received from debtors but that this cash will be received earlier which may alleviate any anticipated cash flow problems.

Example

A business has the following budgeted credit sales and budgeted cash payments:

	Jan £	Feb £	Mar £	Apr £	May £	Jun £	July £
Budgeted sales in £000's	100	120	110	140	150	160	170
Budgeted cash payments in £000's	80	94	108	110	120	135	140

The current credit terms are payment within 60 days and the current payment pattern is that 20% of customers pay during the month following sale, 70% pay two months after the sale and 10% three months after the date of sale.

The company is considering introducing a settlement discount of 2% for payment during the month after sale. This is anticipated to result in 60% of customers paying in the month after sale, 30% two months after the date of sale and 10% three months after the date of sale.

The company anticipates a bank overdraft of £20,000 at the start of April.

(i) Determine the net cash balance at the end of each of the months of April, May and June under the existing credit terms.

(ii) Calculate the effect on the net cash balance at the end of each of the three months if the new policy of offering a settlement discount were introduced from the start of the year.

(iii) Comment on how the new policy affects the net cash balance for each of the three months.

Solution

Under existing policy	April £	May £	June £	July £
RECEIPTS				
Cash from debtors in one month 20%	22,000	28,000	30,000	32,000
Cash from debtors in two months 70%	84,000	77,000	98,000	105,000
Cash from debtors in three months 10%	10,000	12,000	11,000	14,000
Total receipts	116,000	117,000	139,000	151,000
PAYMENTS				
Payment to creditors	110,000	120,000	135,000	140,000
Total payments	110,000	120,000	135,000	140,000
Net cash flow	6,000	(3,000)	4,000	11,000
Opening bank balance	(20,000)	(14,000)	(17,000)	(13,000)
Closing bank balance	(14,000)	(17,000)	(13,000)	(2,000)

Under new policy	April £	May £	June £	July £
RECEIPTS				
Cash from debtors in one month 60%	64,680	82,320	88,200	94,080
Cash from debtors in two months 30%	36,000	33,000	42,000	45,000
Cash from debtors in three months 10%	10,000	12,000	11,000	11,000
Total receipts	110,680	127,320	141,200	150,080
PAYMENTS				
Payment to creditors	110,000	120,000	135,000	140,000
Total payments	110,000	120,000	135,000	140,000
Net cash flow	680	7,320	6,200	10,080
Opening bank balance	(20,000)	(19,320)	(12,000)	(5,800)
Closing bank balance	(19,320)	(12,000)	(5,800)	4,280

Under the new policy of offering the settlement discount, the overdraft is eventually eliminated. This compares to the old policy which would see the overdraft of £20,000 at the start of April and remaining as an overdraft at the end of June.

 Activity 8

A cash budget has been prepared for Maximillian Ltd for the next 4 periods. The budget was prepared based on the following sales volumes and a selling price of £12 per item.

	March (1)	April (2)	May (3)	June (4)
Sales volume	1,300	1,500	1,700	1,900

The pattern of cash receipts used in the budget assumed 50% of sales were received in the month of sale and the remaining 50% in the month following sale.

In the light of current economic trends Maximillian Ltd needs to adjust its cash budget to take account of the following:

• The selling price from period 1 will be reduced by 5% per item

• The pattern of sales receipts changes to 25% of sales received in the month of sale, 30% in the month following sale and the remaining 45% two months after sale.

Complete the table below to show the effect of the changes in values and timing of receipts:

	March	April	May	June
Original value of sales				
Original timing of receipts				
Revised value of sales				
Revised timing of receipts (working)				
Revised timing of receipts				
Increase/(decrease) in receipts				

Maximillian Ltd has managed to negotiate extended payment terms with its suppliers. The original budget was to pay in the month after purchase. The settlement is now split over the 2 months after purchase – 50% is paid in the month after purchase and the remaining the month after that.

	March	April	May	June
Purchases	8,000	8,200	8,400	8,600

Complete the table below to show the effect of the changes in timing of the payments:

	March	April	May	June
Original timing of payments				
Revised timing of payments (working)				
Revised timing of payments				
(Increase)/decrease in payment				

Using the information above on receipts and payments complete the table below to show the effect of the changes on the budgeted bank balance for the months of June, July and August.

	April	May	June
Original net cash flow	5,000	5,300	5,800
Changes in receipts			
Changes in payments			
Revised net cash flow			
Opening bank balance	7,500		
Closing bank balance			

7　Monitoring cash flow

7.1　Introduction

Once a cash flow budget has been drawn up, the management of the business are in a position to plan their working capital requirements. Knowing the business's projected cash position, it is possible to estimate:

- the need for cash and the ability to finance this

- the possible sources from which any shortfall can be financed
- what to do with any surplus cash.

This is covered in the next chapters of this book.

As well as using the cash budget to identify any anticipated surplus or deficit in future periods, it is also important to monitor the actual performance of the business compared to the budgeted performance. This is part of the management process of control whereby the actual cash flows are compared to the budgeted cash flows and any significant variances between the two are highlighted and investigated.

7.2 Comparison of actual to budgeted cash flows

For each line of the cash budget the actual cash flow for each month and for the period in total can be compared to the corresponding budgeted figure. Any major differences should be investigated to determine why the variance happened and to consider how this can be dealt with in terms of future operations or future budgeting.

Example

Given below are the actual and budgeted cash flows for the month of April:

	Actual £	Budget £
Cash sales	6,400	9,000
Receipts from debtors	27,800	34,000
Payments to creditors	(20,500)	(16,700)
Production wages	(3,600)	(3,600)
Administration costs	(2,100)	(2,000)
Capital expenditure	(14,000)	–
Net cash flow	(6,000)	20,700
Opening cash balance	3,200	3,200
Closing cash balance	(2,800)	23,900

What are the significant differences between the actual cash flows for the month and the budgeted cash flows and how might the company have tried to avoid the overdraft balance that actually occurred at the end of the month?

Solution

Cash sales are £2,600 less than budgeted.

Receipts from debtors are £6,200 less than budgeted. Payments to creditors are £3,800 more than budgeted.

There is capital expenditure of £14,000 which was not budgeted for.

Taking these factors all together, this means that the company has an overdraft of £2,800 at the end of the month rather than the healthy budgeted cash balance of almost £24,000.

The company could have tried to avoid the overdraft situation in the following ways:

- Better credit control and collection procedures leading to higher receipts from debtors.

- Delaying payments to creditors or negotiating longer credit terms with the suppliers.

- Postponing the capital expenditure.

- Purchasing the capital items on lease or hire purchase terms rather than outright.

- Finding specific finance for the capital expenditure such as a bank loan.

7.3 Reconciliation of budgeted cash balance to actual cash balance

After determining the variances between the actual cash flows and the budgeted cash for the period then it should be possible to use these differences to reconcile the budgeted cash balance at the end of the period to the actual cash balance. This provides a useful summary to the management of the business for the causes of the unexpected actual position.

Example

Given below are the actual and budgeted cash flows for April from the previous example:

	Actual £	Budget £
Cash sales	6,400	9,000
Receipts from debtors	27,800	34,000
Payments to creditors	(20,500)	(16,700)
Production wages	(3,600)	(3,600)
Administration costs	(2,100)	(2,000)
Capital expenditure	(14,000)	–
Net cash flow	(6,000)	20,700
Opening cash balance	3,200	3,200
Closing cash balance	(2,800)	23,900

Prepare a reconciliation of the budgeted cash balance of £23,900 to the actual overdraft figure of £2,800 at the end of the month.

Solution

Reconciliation of budgeted cash balance to actual cash balance

	£
Budged cash balance at 30 April	23,900
Shortfall in cash sales	(2,600)
Shortfall in receipts from debtors	(6,200)
Additional payments to suppliers	(3,800)
Additional administration costs	(100)
Unbudgeted capital expenditure	(14,000)
Actual overdraft at 30 April	(2,800)

Activity 9

Given below are the actual and budgeted cash flows for the month of October for a business:

	Actual £	Budget £
Receipts from debtors	106,000	132,400
Payments to suppliers	(79,000)	(70,000)
Production wages	(17,500)	(17,000)
Production expenses	(1,500)	(1,000)
Selling expenses	(3,400)	(4,000)
Administration expenses	(4,100)	(4,100)
Dividend	(20,000)	
Net cash flow	(19,500)	36,300
Opening cash balance	10,000	10,000
Closing cash balance	(9,500)	46,300

(a) Reconcile the actual cash balance at the end of October to the budgeted cash balance at that date.

£

Budgeted closing bank balance
Surplus/(Shortfall) in receipts from debtors
(Increase)/decrease in payments to suppliers
(Increase)/decrease in production wages
(Increase)/decrease in production expenses
(Increase)/decrease in selling expenses
Other –

Actual closing bank balance

_____

(b) What action could the organisation have taken to avoid an overdrawn bank balance

    A   Chased customers to pay sooner

    B   Delayed payments to suppliers

    C   Avoided dividend payment

    D   Reduced selling expenses

7.4 Cause of variances between budget and actual cash flow

Variances or differences between budget and actual cash flows can occur for a number of reasons. There are also a variety of courses of action available to minimise adverse variances or benefit from favourable variances.

Listed below are possible causes for adverse variances with possible courses of action.

Reduced receipts from debtors

Lower volume of sales than budgeted

- Increase marketing/advertising
- Reduce price to be competitive
- Offer deals i.e. BOGGOF
- Improve the product

Lower selling price than budgeted

- Check the level of deals being offered by salesmen
- Check competition for their prices

Receipts taking longer to be collected from debtors

- Improve credit control/Outsource debt collection
- Change payment terms in contract
- Offer a settlement discount for early payment

Increased payments

Higher price paid for raw materials

- Negotiate an early payment discount
- Negotiate a trade or bulk discount
- Change supplier

More materials required for production

- Change manufacturing techniques
- Offer bonuses to employees for meeting usage targets
- Investigate product requirement

Increase in labour costs	• Reduce overtime working
	• Offer bonuses to employees for meeting efficiency targets
	• Inexperienced staff take longer so look to increase training
	• Investigate the possibility of mechanisation/computerisation of some tasks or processes
Increase in other costs i.e. electricity, rent etc	• May be little action that can be taken as these are not very controllable by the business. It may be that the original budget did not take into account price rises

Capital expenditure/receipts

| Payment or receipt made | • Make sure the all large items of expenditure are communicated to the budget manager |
| | • There was an unexpected need for new fixed assets so it was not able to be budgeted for |

On the whole favourable variances indicate that a working practice has improved i.e. labour costs are lower than budget; staff are working more efficiently therefore not working as much overtime to meet production or sales demand.

Unfortunately though sometimes a favourable variance may mean that there has been something adverse as well i.e. labour costs are lower than budget; staff are not working as many hours as production or sales demand is lower than predicted. This would therefore require investigation and correction.

Activity 10

Match each cause of a variance listed on the left with a possible course of action from the list on the right.

Receipts are not coming in as planned	Check the competition
Payments are being made late to suppliers	Change supplier
Sales volume has decreased	Outsource credit control
Payments to suppliers have increased in value	Improve staff efficiency
Labour costs have increased	Negotiate an early settlement discount

8 Summary

When preparing cash budgets a lot of forecast information is required, particularly regarding sales forecasts. One method of forecasting the sales figure is to use time series analysis where the trend is determined and this information is then used to forecast future sales. Further methods of forecasting sales is to use anticipated growth of sales and inflation rates to update the current sales figures and produce a forecast or to use index numbers.

The figures in the cash budget are all estimates based upon projected sales figures and assumptions regarding factors such as the payment pattern of debtors and the speed of payment to creditors. Management may be interested in how the net cash position would change if these estimates or assumptions change. This can be determined by various forms of sensitivity analysis. Computer spreadsheets can be used not only to speed up the preparation of cash budgets but also to easily carry out a variety of forms of sensitivity analysis.

As well as using cash budgets in order to plan for anticipated deficits or surpluses, management will also need to compare the actual cash flows for a period to the budgeted cash flows as part of the process of control. Useful information for management will be a reconciliation between the budgeted cash balance at the end of the period and the actual cash balance in order to highlight areas that can be improved in terms of operations or budgeting.

 Test your knowledge

Having completed Chapter 3 you should now be able to attempt:

Practice Activities 14 to 19

Answers to chapter activities

Activity 1

Month	Value	3-month moving total	Trend
Jan	12		
Feb	25	55	18
Mar	18	58	19
Apr	15	63	21
May	30	66	22
Jun	21	70	23
Jul	19	72	24
Aug	32	76	25
Sept	25		

Activity 2

Month	Sales Value (000s)	3 month moving total	Trend
June	770		
July	750	2,430	810
August	910	2,565	855
September	905	2,740	913
October	925	2,700	900
November	870	2,785	928
December	990		

Activity 3

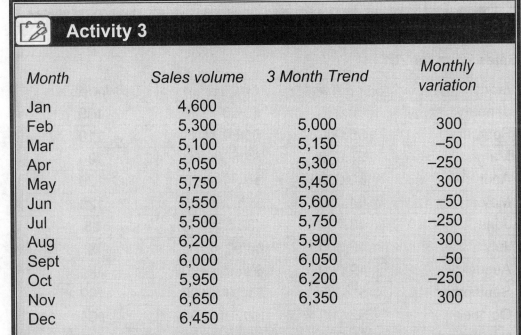

Month	Sales volume	3 Month Trend	Monthly variation
Jan	4,600		
Feb	5,300	5,000	300
Mar	5,100	5,150	−50
Apr	5,050	5,300	−250
May	5,750	5,450	300
Jun	5,550	5,600	−50
Jul	5,500	5,750	−250
Aug	6,200	5,900	300
Sept	6,000	6,050	−50
Oct	5,950	6,200	−250
Nov	6,650	6,350	300
Dec	6,450		

The monthly sales volume trend is an increase of 150 each month

Month	Forecast sales trend	Variation	Forecast sale volume
Mar	6,950	−50	6,900
Apr	7,100	−250	6,850
May	7,250	300	7,550

November's trend is 6,350 therefore this needs to be increased 4 times by 150 to get March's forecast sales trend.

6,350 + (150 × 4) = 6,950

The variation cycle is 300, −50, −250 therefore the variation for March is −50. The variation is negative therefore the sales will be less than the trend.

Activity 4

Sales units for 20Y1

Month	Sales (units)	Calculation	Index
January	50,000	50/50 ×100	100
February	55,000	55/50 ×100	110
March	52,000	52/50 ×100	104
April	60,000	60/50 ×100	120
May	64,000	64/50 × 100	128
June	48,000	48/50 × 100	96
July	46,000	46/50 × 100	92
August	49,000	49/50 × 100	98
September	51,000	51/50 × 100	102
October	52,000	52/50 × 100	104
November	55,000	55/50 × 100	110
December	53,000	53/50 × 100	106

Forecast for 20Y2

Month	Index	Calculation	Forecast sale volume
January	100	100/100 × 52	52,000
February	110	110/100 × 52	57,200
March	104	104/100 × 52	54,080
April	120	120/100 × 52	62,400
May	128	128/100 × 52	66,560
June	96	96/100 × 52	49,920
July	92	92/100 × 52	47,840
August	98	98/100 × 52	50,960
September	102	102/100 × 52	53,040
October	104	104/100 × 52	54,080
November	110	110/100 × 52	57,200
December	106	106/100 × 52	55,120

Activity 5

Answer C

7,800/134 ×162 = £9,430

 Activity 6

Year	Sales revenue	Calculation	Deflated sales revenue
	£	£	£
20X1	486,000	486,000 × 111.8/111.8	486,000
20X2	521,000	521,000 × 111.8/131.9	441,606
20X3	562,000	562,000 × 111.8/145.9	430,648
20X4	604,000	604,000 × 111.8/150.3	449,283
20X5	683,000	683,000 × 111.8/156.3	488,544

 Activity 7

(a) **1% increase in sales**

	April £	May £	June £
Sales (× 1.01)	2,626	3,131	1,616
Increase/(decrease)	26	31	16
New net cash flow	126	381	(284)
Balance b/f	100	226	607
Balance c/f	226	607	323

i.e. a 1% increase in sales results in the bank balance increasing from £250 to £323. This is an increase of £73 (i.e. 29%).

2% decrease in sales

	April £	May £	June £
Sales (× 0.98)	2,548	3,038	1,568
Increase/(decrease)	(52)	(62)	(32)
New net cash flow	48	288	(332)
Balance b/f	100	148	436
Balance c/f	148	436	104

A 2% decrease in sales has not caused the bank balance to become overdrawn but cash has fallen to £104. This is a £146 (i.e. 58%) fall.

 Activity 8

	March	April	May	June
Original value of sales	15,600	18,000	20,400	22,800
Original timing of receipts	7,800	16,800	19,200	21,600
Revised value of sales	14,820	17,100	19,380	21,660
Revised timing of receipts (working)	3,705	4,275 4,446	4,845 5,130 6,669	5,415 5,814 7,695
Revised timing of receipts	3,705	8,721	16,644	18,924
Increase/(decrease) in receipts	(4,095)	(8,079)	(2,566)	(2,676)

	March	April	May	June
Original timing of payments		8,000	8,200	8,400
Revised timing of payments (working)		4,000	4,100 4,000	4,200 4,100
Revised timing of payments		4,000	8,100	8,300
(Increase)/decrease in payment		4,000	100	100

	April	May	June
Original net cash flow	5,000	5,300	5,800
Changes in receipts	(8,079)	(2,556)	(2,676)
Changes in payments	4,000	100	100
Revised net cash flow	921	2,844	3,024
Opening bank balance	7,500	8,421	11,265
Closing bank balance	8,421	11,265	14,289

 Activity 9

(a) **Reconciliation of budgeted cash balance to actual cash balance**

	£
Budgeted cash balance	46,300
Shortfall in receipts from debtors	(26,400)
Additional payments to suppliers	(9,000)
Additional production wages	(500)
Additional production expenses	(500)
Shortfall in selling expenses	600
Unbudgeted dividend	(20,000)
Actual overdraft	(9,500)

(b) Answer C

   A   Chased customers to pay sooner – would cover overdraft but the company does not have complete control on when the debtors pay

   B   Delayed payments to suppliers – would not remove the overdraft

   C   Avoided dividend payment – covers overdraft and company has more control over the payment of dividends

   D   Reduced selling expenses – not required

Activity 10

Receipts are not coming in as planned	Outsource credit control
Payments are being made late to suppliers	Negotiate an early settlement discount
Sales volume has decreased	Check the competition
Payments to suppliers have increased in value	Change supplier
Labour costs have increased	Improve staff efficiency

Raising finance

Introduction

In an earlier chapter we saw that one of the purposes of preparing a cash flow forecast was in order for the management of a company to be able to forecast whether there is likely to be any cash surplus or cash deficit in the future periods. If a cash deficit is forecast then management will need to make arrangements well in advance for how to deal with that deficit. In this chapter we consider the use of overdrafts and loans as forms of finance that can be raised to deal with any known shortage of cash at a future date, how that finance can be arranged and the most appropriate form of finance for specific situations.

KNOWLEDGE

Identify statutory and other regulations relating to the management of cash balances in different types of organisations (1.4)

Explain how an organisation can raise finance from a bank through overdrafts and loans, and the basic terms and conditions associated with each of these types of financing (2.2)

SKILLS

Observe the organisation's financial regulations and security procedures (3.1)

Manage cash, overdrafts and loans in order to maintain an adequate level of liquidity in line with cash forecasts (3.3)

Anticipate cash requirements and arrange overdraft and loan facilities on the most favourable terms available (3.4)

CONTENTS

1   The need to raise finance

2   Short-term debt finance

3   Long-term debt finance

4   Choosing the form of finance

1 The need to raise finance

1.1 Introduction

Any business will have an initial amount of capital which is either contributed by the owner or, in the case of a company, is issued share capital. However at various stages in the business life cycle the management may find that there is a need to raise additional finance.

1.2 Reasons for additional finance

There are many reasons why a business may need to raise additional finance but the most common are:

- to fund working capital
- to increase working capital
- to reduce creditors
- to purchase fixed assets
- to acquire another business.

The need to raise the finance may be highlighted by a deficit in the cash budget, by management decisions regarding investment in fixed assets or by the business strategy of growth by acquisition.

1.3 Funding working capital

One of the most common reasons for additional finance which is normally highlighted by a deficit in the cash budget is in order to fund working capital. The working capital of a business will have an operating cycle (see chapter 1) which is effectively the period between the payment of money for goods and the receipt of money from debtors. If creditors are being paid more quickly than money is being received from debtors then at some time it is likely that the business will require funds to tide them over until the money from the debtors is received.

1.4 Increasing working capital

After a period of operating, a business may find that it needs an increase in its working capital. This may be due to **increased sales turnover** which in turn requires **increases in stocks and debtors**. The business may be able to gain additional credit from its trade creditors but in the absence of that may have to raise funds to finance this increase. Care should be taken in such circumstances to ensure that the business is not overtrading (see chapter 1).

Alternatively the additional finance required might be due to an increase in debtors. This might be due to inefficiencies in the credit control of the business or it may be that increased credit has had to be offered to customers in order to keep their custom in a competitive market or to increase market share and sales turnover.

Often additional finance might be required due to an increase in stock levels which is not associated with a general increase in turnover. Such a stock increase will normally only be temporary and could be due to:

- taking advantage of an attractive price by placing a bulk order

- building up stocks in advance of a peak period in a seasonal business

- receipt of a large order from a customer.

1.5 Reduction of creditors

A business may need to reduce its trade creditors either in order to **take advantage of settlement discounts** or due to the fact that trade creditors may be pressing the business for quicker payment for their own reasons. This reduction in trade credit will need to be funded by some other source of finance. If creditors are to be paid earlier, then the cash to do this will have to be found.

Equally additional finance might be required for the short term to fund payments such as **quarterly VAT payments** or the **annual Corporation Tax payment**.

1.6 Purchase of fixed assets

Not only will a business require enough cash to pay its creditors and expenses, such as wages, when they fall due, but most businesses will also need to **invest in additional or replacement fixed assets** on a fairly regular basis. In many cases a business will not have enough cash to purchase the fixed assets required to maintain or expand operations out of cash and will therefore need to raise finance in order to fund the purchase.

1.7 Acquisition of another business

Many businesses have a policy of growth by acquisition of other businesses. Such a major amount of expenditure will almost always require funding by some form of external finance.

In general terms the types of finance available can be categorised as:

- short term – anything up to 3 years

- long term – over 3 years.

In the rest of this chapter we will consider bank overdrafts as an example of short term finance and bank loans as examples of long term finance. A rule of thumb is that the time scale of the finance should match the time scale of the reason for the finance. Therefore if the finance is required for working capital reasons then the finance should be short term whereas if the finance is required for longer term investment in fixed assets or another business then the appropriate finance may be medium or long term.

2   Short-term debt finance

2.1   Introduction

Short-term debt finance is used for:

(a) temporary working capital

(b) bridging finance for assets being financed from the sale of existing assets, and

(c) purchase of short-lived assets.

The most common type of short-term finance is a bank overdraft.

2.2   Bank overdraft

Bank overdrafts are most often negotiated for a **fixed period** in terms of a **maximum available** facility. In other words, the bank undertakes to advance anything up to, say £50,000, and the business can take advantage of the facility as and when it needs to. The **interest** will generally be at a **variable** rate, calculated on a day-to-day basis with reference to the bank's base rate. The principal advantage of an overdraft is **flexibility**. The business only pays interest on the amount actually drawn, although there may be an additional flat charge of perhaps 0.25% on the maximum facility.

Overdrafts are (technically) **repayable on demand** and should never be regarded as substitutes for adequate medium term finance.

2.3   Short-term bank loan

A term loan with a bank is a loan for a **fixed amount**, for an **agreed period** on pre-arranged terms. The loan will be governed by formal documentation which will include:

- the term of the loan

- the interest rate

- the way in which the interest is charged

- the repayment date/dates

- any security required for the loan

- any covenants attached to the loan.

Term loans can be for virtually any period and the repayment terms can be negotiated with the bank:

- **Interest** rates may be **fixed or variable**.

- There are a variety of methods of repaying interest and capital (see later in the chapter).

- The loan can be drawn upon in stages, e.g. 50% now and 50% in three months' time.

3 Long-term debt finance

3.1 Introduction

On the whole long-term debt finance should be used to fund the purchase of assets with a **three- to ten-year life** such as plant and machinery. However it can also be useful to fund a medium term deficit in working capital.

3.2 Bank loans

An obvious source of finance for say the purchase of major fixed assets is a bank loan. The **term** of the loan should not exceed the **life of the asset** being purchased and will normally be approximately the same as the asset's useful life. The **interest** on the loan will either be **fixed or variable**. If the interest is variable then the interest charged will depend upon market rates of interest and will normally be a certain percentage above the bank's base rate or the London Inter-Bank Offered Rate (LIBOR).

3.3 Security

In some cases the bank may only be prepared to advance the money on the basis of some security given by the business. Security can be in the form of a fixed charge or a floating charge.

Definition

A fixed charge is where the security is a specific and identifiable asset or group of assets.

The bank would have the right to sell this asset if the business defaults on the loan repayments.

 Definition

A floating charge is where the security is supplied by a group of assets to the relevant value of the business such as debtors or stock which will be constantly changing.

If the business defaults on the loan then the bank has the right to however much of those assets the business has at the time.

 Activity 1

A fixed charge is security offered by a changing group of assets and a floating charge is security offered by a static asset.

True or false?

3.4 Long-term loan and working capital

In most cases a bank loan is most appropriate for the purchase of major assets which will hopefully provide income over the loan period out of which the loan interest and repayments can be made. However in some cases it may be necessary to raise a loan to finance a working capital deficit.

For example suppose that a company has consistently had an overdraft of between £20,000 and £30,000 for the last two years. This would appear to be part of the permanent working capital of the business and is known as the hardcore overdraft. Overdraft finance tends to be at a higher rate of interest than loan finance as it is harder to monitor from the bank's perspective and is more volatile. Therefore this company might convert the hardcore overdraft into say a £20,000 five-year loan which will be paid off over the period but which should reduce the amount of additional overdraft finance required.

4 Choosing the form of finance

4.1 Introduction

Bank overdraft and bank loans each have different characteristics and different costs and it is vital that the most appropriate and cheapest form of finance is chosen to meet the funding requirements of each situation.

In some situations a specific form of finance will be clearly the most appropriate. However, in many cases, the choice that must be made by the accounting function is the choice between financing by bank overdraft or by taking out a term loan.

4.2 Overdraft or bank loan

In general terms the financing method should be matched to the life of the asset for which the financing is required. Therefore, in most cases, an **overdraft** is most suitable for increased **working capital** requirements and a **loan** is more suitable for the purchase of **fixed assets** or another business. However, you do need to appreciate the advantages and disadvantages of each of these two main sources of finance.

4.3 Advantages of a bank overdraft

A bank overdraft as a source of short term funding has a number of advantages:

- **Flexibility**. An overdraft facility is the amount that the business could borrow from the bank in the form of an overdraft. However, the full facility does not need to be used and therefore the precise amount of funding required does not need to be estimated. For example, a business may have been granted an overdraft facility of £50,000 but currently only requires £30,000 of regular overdraft finance.

- **Cost**. Although the interest rate on an overdraft may be higher than that which could be negotiated on a loan, the important point about overdraft **interest is** that it is **calculated daily** on the amount of the actual overdraft each day rather than on a fixed amount as would be the interest on a loan.

- **Short-term**. Technically an overdraft is repayable on demand and therefore should only be used to fund short-term working capital requirements. The benefit of this is that when the short-term funding requirement is over the overdraft facility is simply not required. There is no necessity to negotiate paying off a loan early or incurring a penalty for early repayment.

4.4 Disadvantages of a bank overdraft

However, there are also some drawbacks to the use of overdraft finance:

- **Repayable on demand**. Technically the overdraft is repayable on demand and if the business is seen by the bank as not meeting its cash flow forecasts or business plan then the bank could cancel the overdraft facility and require any outstanding amount to be repaid possibly causing severe cash flow repercussions for the business.

- **Increasing the facility**. Once an overdraft facility has been agreed with the bank it may be difficult to persuade the bank to increase that facility if additional finance is required.

- **Short term**. As the overdraft is repayable on demand, it is only really suitable for the financing of short term assets such as investment in additional working capital rather than longer term situations such as the purchase of fixed assets or acquisition of another business.

4.5 Advantages of loan finance

The main advantage of loan finance is that it can be tailored to meet the requirements of the borrower. It can be taken out for a period which matches the assets which it is financing and the repayment terms can be negotiated to match with the cash flows from the asset or the other business cash flows.

4.6 Disadvantages of loan finance

- **Interest rate**. If the interest on the loan is fixed rate then this is often more expensive than an overdraft or a variable rate loan.

- **Security**. The bank will normally require some form of security for the loan, either a fixed or a floating charge.

- **Restrictions**. The bank may impose certain restrictions or covenants which will limit the freedom of action of the management of the business, for example restrictions on payment of dividends or on other forms of finance taken out by the business.

- **Interest charged**. On a loan the interest charge is based upon the full amount of the loan, whereas with a bank overdraft interest is only charged on the amount of the overdraft facility actually being used at the current time.

Activity 2

Which of the following best describes the main features of an overdraft?

A   Interest rates are low; it is available for as long as required; it is useful for capital purchases.

B   Interest rates are low; it is payable on demand; it is useful for capital purchases.

C   Interest rates are low; repayments can be negotiated; it is useful for capital purchases.

D   Interest rates are high; repayments can be negotiated; it is a short-term form of finance.

E   Interest rates are high; it is repayable on demand; it is a short-term form of finance.

F   Interest rates are high; it is available for as long as required; it is a long-term form of finance.

Which of the following best describes the main features of a bank loan?

A   Interest rates are low; it is available for as long as required; it is useful for capital purchases.

B   Interest rates are low; it is payable on demand; it is useful for capital purchases.

C   Interest rates are low; repayments can be negotiated; it is useful for capital purchases.

D   Interest rates are high; repayments can be negotiated; it is a short-term form of finance.

E   Interest rates are high; it is repayable on demand; it is a short-term form of finance.

F   Interest rates are high; it is available for as long as required; it is a long-term form of finance.

Activity 3

Steinburgs are planning to expand their manufacturing facilities. The expansion plans require new machinery at a cost of £60,000 and a working capital injection of £10,000.

There are 3 different options for funding the expansion:

Option 1

- A bank loan of £60,000 secured on the new machinery. Capital repayments are to be made of equal amounts over 3 years. The interest rate is fixed at 4% per annum calculated on the capital balance outstanding at the beginning of each year.

- An arrangement equal to 0.5% of the bank loan is payable at the beginning of the loan term.

- The bank is also offering an overdraft facility of £15,000 which attracts an annual interest rate of 13%. Steinburgs believe that they will have an average overdraft of £8,000 for the first 7 months of the first year.

Option 2

- A bank loan of £80,000 secured on the assets of the partnership. Capital repayments are to be made over 3 years, with a 3 month payment holiday at the beginning of the loan term.

- The interest rate is fixed at 8% per annum for the first 2 years and will then revert to a variable interest rate 3% above the base rate.

- An arrangement fee equal to 0.9% of the bank loan is payable at the beginning of the loan term.

- No overdraft facility will be required.

Option 3

- Steinburgs two owners each take out a personal secured loan for £35,000 repayable over 4 years at an interest rate of 4%. These monies will then be loaned to the partnership as increased capital. Interest of 7% per annum is payable by the business to the two owners.

- No overdraft facility will be required.

Required

Calculate the cost of each of the above options for the first year. Which of the 3 methods would you recommend?

	Loan Interest £	Arrangement fee £	Overdraft interest £	Total cost £
Option 1				
Option 2				
Option 3				

Recommendation:

5 Summary

There are many choices facing a business that needs to raise finance but it is important that the right choice of the form of finance is made. This will start with an initial consideration of the reason for the additional finance. If it is due to the need for increased working capital then a form of short-term or possibly loan finance would be most appropriate. If the finance is required for the purchase of fixed assets then long-term finance to match with the life of the asset is probably the best option.

Test your knowledge

Having completed Chapter 4 you should now be able to attempt:

Practice Activities 20 to 24

Answers to chapter activities

Activity 1

False

A fixed charge is security offered by a specific assets

A floating charge is security offered by a group of assets

Activity 2

Which of the following best describes the main features of an overdraft?

E   Interest rates are high; it is repayable on demand; it is a short-term form of finance.

Which of the following best describes the main features of a bank loan?

C   Interest rates are low; repayments can be negotiated; it is useful for capital purchases.

Activity 3

	Loan Interest £	Arrangement fee £	Overdraft interest £	Total cost £
Option 1	2,400	300	607	3,307
Option 2	6,400	720	0	7,120
Option 3	4,900	0	0	4,900

Recommendation: Option 1 as it is the cheapest

Investing surplus funds

5

Introduction

In this chapter we will consider the ways in which any cash surplus a business may have can be invested and the factors that should be considered for determining the best type of investment.

KNOWLEDGE
Explain how government monetary policies affect an organisation's treasury function (1.1)
Describe how an organisation's principles of cash management will be determined by their specific financial regulations, guidelines and security procedures (1.3)
Identify statutory and other regulations relating to the management of cash balances in different types of organisations (1.4)
Explain different types of investment, the risks and terms and conditions associated with them, including: certificates of deposit; government securities; local authority short term loans; shares (2.3)
Identify the ways to manage risk and exposure when investing, to minimise potential losses to the organisation (3.6)

CONTENTS
1 General requirements for investing
2 Types of investment
3 Managing the cash balance
4 Dealing with cash

SKILLS

Observe the organisation's financial regulations and security procedures (3.1)

Invest surplus funds according to organisational policy and within defined financial authorisation limits (3.5)

1 General requirements for investing

1.1 Introduction

Cash budgets, as we have seen, are meant to reveal, among other things, the **amount** of any surplus funds available to the company for short-term investment. Opportunities like this should always be taken; money **invested just overnight will be worth more than money left idle**. Surplus cash will therefore call for an investment decision. This should be based on general principles as well as factors specific to the particular circumstances. The general factors to consider are:

- **Size** of funds available for investment.

- **Length** of time for which funds are available.

- **Certainty** of surplus funds and accuracy of cash budget.

- **Return** on invested funds: Is it adequate? Does it compensate for the risk involved?

- **Risk** and variability of return from the investment if held for the full intended duration.

- Whether there is any possibility that the cash may be required prematurely to make unexpected payments and whether there would be any costs in the event of an early termination.

- Risks associated with early termination. A security which provides a fixed, risk-free return if held for the full term may prove risky if terminated early.

- The funds should be placed with creditworthy borrowers.

- **Realisation**. In some circumstances it may be important that the investment can be realised easily. It provides a company with a reserve, or safety margin, in its cash planning.

The overall aim should be to secure the maximum interest possible, consistent with a satisfactory level of risk and the required degree of liquidity. The investing company has to balance the expected interest with the risks involved.

The differences between the various forms of investment opportunities arise over rates of interest, periods to maturity, realisation and risk.

1.2 Main factors to consider

The three main factors that should be considered when determining how to deal with surplus funds are:

- risk
- return
- liquidity

1.3 Risk and return

As a general rule risk and return are related. The **higher the risk** of an investment the **higher will be its return**. A business that has surplus funds to invest will wish those funds to earn a good profit or return but what is also paramount is the safety of the asset.

1.4 Risk

When cash is invested there are two potential risks. Firstly the risk that the **value of the investment will fall**, the capital risk, and secondly the risk that **the return from the investment will be lower than expected** due to changes in market rates.

 Example

A business has £10,000 of surplus cash to invest for a period of one month until it is needed to pay the quarterly VAT bill. The money could be paid into a bank deposit account earning 0.4% interest per month or it could be invested in shares purchased through a broker.

Consider the risks of these two options. Solution

If the money is paid into the bank deposit account there is virtually no risk at all (provided that the bank is creditworthy!). The withdrawal in one month's time will total:

$$£10,000 + (0.4\% \times £10,000) = £10,040$$

The investment has earned £40 of income for the business.

If the £10,000 were to be invested in shares then in one month's time the share value may have increased to say £13,000, in which case the shares could be sold for that amount earning £3,000 of profit. However it is also possible that the share values have fallen and the shares can only be sold for £7,500 in one month's time meaning not only that a loss has been made but also that there is no longer enough cash available to pay the VAT bill.

1.5 Return and liquidity

When any surplus cash is invested it is important to ensure that it can be realised when needed. The ease of realisation will be reflected in the return that the investment gives. If the cash surplus is certain and the business is certain that it will not need the cash for a period then it will usually be able to earn a higher return than an investment where the cash can be realised immediately.

For example the interest earned on a bank deposit account which requires a month's notice for any withdrawal will be higher than the interest on a deposit account where the funds can be withdrawn at any time.

1.6 Treasury activities and risk

Many large companies have a separate **treasury department** which deals with **investing of surplus funds and raising of finance**. In smaller companies this role normally falls to the accounts department. Whoever is in charge of this function, care must be taken to ensure that although **surplus cash is invested profitably**, excessive risks are not taken. There are many highly speculative and highly risky financial instruments on the market which although they may reap very high returns can also have huge losses.

The aim of the treasury activities in a trading company is to earn a **reasonable return on any surplus cash but not to speculate**.

1.7 Organisational rules and procedures

Many companies will have regulations and procedures to ensure that the liquidity of the business is safeguarded. For example that a certain amount of cash must be available immediately at any point in time, that investments in certain types of instrument may be limited to a financial amount, that surplus funds might only be allowed to be invested in certain specified types of investment or that all investments must be convertible into cash within a certain number of days. These procedures, regulations and limits must be followed at all times.

KAPLAN PUBLISHING

The Government can affect an organisation's treasury function by controlling the supply of money and interest rates. The Government has passed the responsibility of interest rates to The Bank of England:

- If interest rates are low economic growth should be stimulated but higher inflation rates will follow.

- If interest rates are high then inflation reduces but investment and economic growth can be stifled.

The interest rate position will impact on what a business decides to invest in as this impact on the level of return an investment makes.

2 Types of investment

2.1 Bank and building society deposit accounts

One of the **safest and simplest** forms of investment for surplus cash is to pay it into a high street bank or building society deposit account. There are a wide variety of such accounts available although the **interest rate**, particularly for small sums is generally **quite low**. There are high interest deposit accounts for larger amounts, for example provided that there is always a balance of, say, at least £5,000 in the account, and the interest rate on these is higher. **Access to the cash is usually immediate** and therefore useful if cash requirements are not known for certain.

For cash that is definitely not going to be required in the near future there are deposits that can be made for a fixed term of up to three months at a variable rate of interest which is linked to money market rates. This will normally yield a higher rate of return due to the lesser liquidity.

2.2 Government securities

 Definition

Government securities or gilt-edged securities are fixed interest securities issued by the Government and available for purchase.

Government securities are also known as gilt-edged securities or gilts and they are available for investment. They are normally **fixed interest** securities and they can be **bought and sold through a broker.**

Government stocks are **fairly low risk** and **very marketable** ensuring that they are a popular form of investment for companies.

2.3   Local Authority Bonds

 Definition

These are certificates issued by individual local authorities and backed by the government.

As there is a less active market in local authority debt and their security is not considered to be quite as good as government securities, Local Authority Bills do tend to have **higher yields than central government securities.**

2.4   Certificates of deposit

 Definition

A certificate of deposit (CD) is issued by a bank or building society which certifies that a certain sum, usually a minimum of £50,000, has been deposited with it to be repaid on a specific date.

The term can range from **seven days to five years** but is usually for six months. CDs are negotiable instruments, they can be bought and sold, therefore if the **holder does not want to wait until the maturity date the CD can be sold in the money market.**

CDs offer a **good rate of interest** and are **highly marketable**. The advantage to companies of investment in a CD is that they can be liquidated at any time at the current market rate. The market in CDs is large and active therefore they are an ideal method for investing large cash surpluses.

2.5   Shares

Shares in companies can be bought as an investment. Shares are bought and sold through a **broker for a fee**. Whilst being a share holder the company/person may receive **dividends** from the company they have invested in.

Share prices can fluctuate depending on either or both the company and general market performance. If a company is achieving good profits and has a good reputation then the return possible from shares is higher than that of the other options discussed. Conversely if confidence in the company or in the general market drops then the loss can also be significant. Due to this shares are considered to be the **most risky** of investment opportunities.

Activity 1

What type of investment do the following describe:

Certificates issued by local authorities and backed by the government. They can be traded on a market. They are considered to be a low risk investment.

A   Certificates of deposit

B   Government securities

C   Local authority loans

D   Bank deposit account

Interest rates are fixed and these types of securities are considered to be low risk because they are backed by the government.

A   Certificates of deposit

B   Government securities

C   Local authority loans

D   Bank deposit account

Certificates issued by banks that certify that an amount of money has been deposited and will be repaid at a specific date in the future. They can be traded on a market. They are considered to be a low risk investment.

A   Certificates of deposit

B   Government securities

C   Local authority loans

D   Bank deposit account

3   Managing the cash balance

3.1   Regulations and procedures

We have seen that the person responsible for managing the cash balances of a business needs to be aware of a great deal of information in order to decide how to best to do this.

That person must also have regard to the organisation's regulations and procedures. Some companies may have a policy of maintaining a minimum balance of, say, £50,000 of instantly available cash and a reserve of £100,000 available, say, within a month.

3.2 Monitoring and control

In order to manage the cash balance effectively, the treasury manager needs information about both the long-term and short-term cash flow figures. From the cash budget, the future can be predicted. However, the day-to-day balance needs to be monitored and controlled to ensure the actual balance approximates to the budgeted figures and is not in deficit.

The company's systems need to be looked at every day to ensure sufficient funds are available. The timing of the cash flows needs to be ascertained day by day to ensure money is banked quickly and prior to large cheques being written to suppliers, etc. Short-term daily cash flows are as important to the company's liquidity as the longer-term forecasts.

3.3 Cash not required

In some instances a significant cash surplus may arise for which a business has no foreseeable use. In such circumstances the cash should be **returned to the shareholders by way of either a dividend or a share repurchase.**

3.4 Investments and risk

We saw earlier in the chapter that there are two main types of risk with investments – capital risk and return risk. When investing in short-term investments it will be necessary to consider these risks and to take into account any expected changes in the economic and financial environment. Of particular concern will be anticipated changes in interest rates.

3.5 Fixed rate and variable rate investments

Some short-term investments will have variable rates of interest. For example, many **bank deposit accounts** have **variable** rates of interest which means that if the bank base rate goes up or down the interest earned on the deposit will also increase or decrease.

However, many other types of investment, such as **fixed rate deposit accounts and gilt edged securities**, are **fixed** rate investments. This means that if the general rate of interest changes there is no change in the interest paid on these investments. However, this does not mean that potential changes in interest rates can be ignored.

3.6 Effect on investments of changes in interest rates

If an investment is made in a **fixed rate deposit account** and interest rates were expected to change then this would have **no effect on the amount deposited**. The principal amount invested will always remain the same and this is the amount that will be repaid at the end of the term of the investment no matter what happens to interest rates.

However, an investment in **fixed rate gilts** is rather different. These are marketable securities and, as such, their **market value will fluctuate** with changes in underlying interest rates or the base rate. If a business has invested in gilts and the **interest rate increases** then the **value of the gilt will fall** in order to ensure that the yield is in line with general interest rates. Conversely, if the base rate of interest is decreased then the market value of the gilts will increase. Therefore, the person responsible for such investments should take account of expected changes in economic and financial conditions.

 Activity 2

Four possible investment options are available:

Option 1

Investment of £60,000 required, there is a 90 day notice period, risk has been assessed as medium due to the inclusion of some shares in the portfolio and the interest rate is 5% per annum.

Option 2

Investment should be between £80,000 and £40,000, there is a 30 day notice period, interest is 3%, risk has been assessed as low as there is no inclusion of shares.

Option 3

Investment portfolio consists of stocks and shares so is high risk but with a projected interest rate of 8%. There is a minimum investment of £35,000 required and a 45 day notice period exists.

Option 4

A low risk investment opportunity with a guaranteed return of 2.5%, the minimum investment required is £40,000 and 10 working days notice must be given for withdrawals.

The treasury department has the following policy for investing surplus funds:

It must be possible to access the cash invested within 45 days

The maximum investment amount is £45,000

The interest rate must be 2.5% above base rate, which is currently 0.5%

The investment must be low risk

Complete the table below and decide which policy can be invested in, if any

	Convertible within 45 days?	Investment £45,000 or below?	Interest rate 2.5% above base rate?	Low risk?	Invest?
Option 1	X	X	✓	X	X
Option 2	✓	✓	✓	✓	✓
Option 3	X	✓	✓	X	X
Option 4	✓	✓	X	✓	X

4 Dealing with cash

4.1 Introduction

At the start of this chapter it was argued that cash is an idle asset and ideally should be invested immediately to earn interest even if this is for a very short term, such as overnight. However, there are many businesses in the retail sector, or even manufacturing businesses with a retail outlet, which will necessarily have to deal with potentially large amounts of cash on a daily basis before it can be banked or otherwise invested.

4.2 Security of cash

Obviously cash is a highly risky asset to be holding on the business premises as it can so easily be misappropriated or stolen. Therefore, for any cash based business or part of a business there must be strict procedures and policies which must be followed to ensure that the cash and cheques taken from customers are secure and are **banked as quickly as possible and intact.**

4.3 Security procedures for cash

Any business dealing with cash must have basic security procedures in place.

The main ones that must be followed are:

- **Physical safeguards.** The cash taken must at all times be kept safe and only accessible to authorised individuals. This means that cash should be kept under lock and key either in a cash box or in a lockable till. Only authorised individuals should have access to the keys.

- **Valid payment.** If cheques are accepted as payment then they must be supported by a valid cheque guarantee card. If credit cards are accepted, authorisation must be sought for payments which exceed the limit.

- **Reconciliation.** A list of all cash, cheques and credit card payments taken during the day must be kept and this must be reconciled at the end of the day to the amount of cash in the till or cash box. The list may be manual as each sale is made or may be automatically recorded on the till roll as each sale is rung in. The reconciliation should be carried out by someone other than the person responsible for making the sales. Any discrepancies between the amount of cash taken during the day and the amount left at the end of the day must be investigated.

- **Banking.** The receipts should be banked intact and promptly each day. This not only ensures the physical safety of the cash in the bank and that it cannot be used by employees for unauthorised purposes, but also that it is earning the business the maximum amount of interest in the bank account. All cash should be banked as soon as possible but if it is not to be banked until the following day, then either the cash must be left in a locked safe overnight or in the bank's overnight safe.

- **Recording.** The paying-in slip for the bank should be made out by someone other than the person paying the money into the bank and should be reconciled to the till records for the day.

5 Summary

If a business has a short-term surplus of funds then these should be invested rather than remaining as idle cash which is not earning any income for the business. The main factors to consider when determining the type of investment are the risk, return and liquidity of the investment. Typical suitable investments for short-term funds are bank and building society deposit accounts, government securities, local authority stocks, certificates of deposit, and bills of exchange.

If a business deals with cash sales then management should ensure that basic security measures for the cash are in place.

 Test your knowledge

Having completed Chapter 5 you should now be able to attempt:

Practice Activities 25 to 26

Answers to chapter activities

 Activity 1

What type of investment do the following describe:

Certificates issued by local authorities and backed by the government. They can be traded on a market. They are considered to be a low risk investment.

C Local authority loans

Interest rates are fixed and these types of securities are considered to be low risk because they are backed by the government.

B Government securities

Certificates issued by banks that certify that an amount of money has been deposited and will be repaid at a specific date in the future. They can be traded on a market. They are considered to be a low risk investment.

A Certificates of deposit

 Activity 2

	Convertible within 45 days?	Investment £45,000 or below?	Interest rate 2.5% above base rate?	Low risk?	Invest?
Option 1	N	N	Y	N	N
Option 2	Y	Y	Y	Y	Y
Option 3	Y	Y	Y	N	N
Option 4	Y	Y	N	Y	N

UK banking system

Introduction

The effective management of cash is not something that can be undertaken in isolation or without an awareness of the general financial environment in which organisations operate.

It is important that you are aware of how the banking sector is structured, the relationship between different financial institutions and understand that legal relationships exist between lenders and borrowers.

The CMGT assessment tasks may contain some technical financial terms to add reality to a task. This chapter aims to explain some of the more common terms.

KNOWLEDGE	CONTENTS
Explain how government monetary policies affect an organisation's treasury functions (1.1)	1 The UK banking system 2 The Bank of England 3 The money markets 4 Government monetary policies

1 The UK banking system

1.1 Introduction

There will always be individuals, partnerships, companies and governments with surplus funds. They will want to invest their excess funds to earn a return.

Similarly, there will always be entities without enough funds. For example, an individual might want to buy a car or a house, a company might want to undertake an ambitious expansion project, or a government might want to buy an expensive weapons system.

The financial system brings both groups together; its intermediaries act as links in the chains joining savers and borrowers. The system is seen at its simplest when individuals deposit their savings at the bank, which then lends the money on to others, but the path can get much more complicated.

1.2 Financial intermediation

Why are the intermediaries needed? Why don't the savers and borrowers get together directly and save the costs which the intermediaries involve? The reason is that financial intermediation brings benefits as follows.

- **'Maturity transformation'** occurs, in which deposits by customers, usually short term, and are lent out to borrowers for much longer periods of time.

- The **risk profile** of a saver is reduced. If financial intermediaries did not exist, a person or organisation with money to lend would have to seek out a potential borrower, who might eventually default. An intermediary is likely to aggregate the deposits of individual depositors for the purpose of granting fewer but more substantial advances, whilst reducing or eliminating the risk of default to savers.

- Intermediaries also provide **considerable benefits to borrowers**, who might otherwise have difficulty locating potential savers who are willing to lend appropriate amounts of funds at reasonable interest rates. Moreover, the use of a financial institution will provide **greater flexibility for borrowers** in that they almost certainly will be permitted to repay loans earlier than originally specified if circumstances permit, or reschedule debts if they have cash flow problems. It is unlikely that, with direct saving and lending, these provisions would be possible.

1.3 Types of financial institutions

There are many different types of financial institutions that play some role in the operation of securities and other capital markets. Some act solely in the role of intermediary, collecting money from investors and passing it on to borrowers; others act as investors/borrowers in their own right. We shall now look at some of the most common types of institution:

- brokers – stock and money

- banks – clearing and merchant

- institutional investors – pension funds, insurance companies, investment and unit trusts

- venture capitalists.

1.4 Brokers

Brokers, in their purest form, act as **agents for investors** who wish to buy or sell shares or funds. They seek out a source or outlet for the required shares or funds and act as a go between in settling price and other terms of the deal. Their profits are generally made by commission and fees.

1.5 Banks

There are two main types of banks in the UK: primary and secondary banks. **Primary banks** are those which operate the **money transmission service** in the economy, the banks which operate cheque accounts and deal with cheque clearing. These are often known as the **commercial banks, retail banks or clearing banks.**

The **secondary banks** consist of a wide range of **merchant banks**, other British banks and foreign banks in the UK. They do not tend to take part in the cheque clearing system.

1.6 Types of deposit

Banks take deposits from customers.

The banks offer a variety of deposit facilities to their customers, one useful distinction being between retail deposits and wholesale deposits.

1.7 Retail deposits

Those banks which operate an extensive branch network obtain a substantial proportion of their sterling resources as retail deposits: **current account deposits** held by individuals or organisations in connection with their ordinary payments and receipts, and other **interest-bearing deposits** held as a supplementary store of liquidity. Retail banking is the **traditional high street banking** with relatively small deposits from and loans to customers.

1.8   Wholesale deposits

Wholesale deposits are **large interest-bearing deposits** – usually of at least £50,000 – on which the interest rate is negotiated. Deposits may be received directly from customers or indirectly through money brokers. The market is very competitive and the rate paid for funds is generally identical for institutions of the same standing. Sources of wholesale deposits include institutions at home and abroad, large companies, non-bank financial institutions and other banks with temporary surplus funds.

The **certificate of deposit (CD) is a particular type of wholesale deposit**. The CD is a document issued by a bank certifying that a deposit has been made with that bank which is repayable to the bearer on surrender of the certificate at maturity. A CD is a negotiable instrument so that, while the bank has a deposit for a fixed term, the depositor has the option of obtaining cash before maturity by selling the certificate in the market.

1.9   Lending facilities

The banks offer a variety of lending facilities to their customers with terms varying according to the type of lending and customer involved.

(a)   Companies are offered overdraft and term lending, syndicated loan finance and services such as instalment credit, leasing and factoring which are often provided through subsidiaries.

(b)   Personal customers get overdraft and bridging finance, personal loans, revolving credit and budget accounts, instalment credit (often through subsidiaries) and credit card finance.

1.10   Relationship of the banker and customer

There are in fact **four main contractual relationships** between the banker and the customer.

The **debtor/creditor relationship** where the customer deposits his money with the bank and the bank becomes the debtor and the customer, the creditor. If the customer's account is overdrawn, however, the bank becomes the creditor and the customer the debtor.

There are a number of essential areas in this element of the contract:

- The bank must receive cheques for the customer's account.

- The bank borrows the customer's deposits and undertakes to repay them.

- The bank will only cease to do business with the customer with reasonable notice.

- The bank is not liable to pay until the customer demands payment.

- The customer exercises reasonable care when writing cheques.

The **bailor/bailee relationship** concerns the bank accepting the customer's property for storage in its safe deposit. The bank undertakes to take reasonable care to safeguard the property against loss or damage and then re-deliver it only to the customer or someone authorised by the customer.

The **principal/agent relationship** where, for example, the customer pays a crossed cheque into the bank, the bank acts as agent when presenting the cheque for payment and paying the proceeds into the customer's account.

The **mortgagor/mortgagee relationship** exists where the bank asks the customer to secure a loan with a charge over the customer's assets. If the customer does not repay the loan then the bank can sell the asset and use the proceeds to pay off the loan.

1.11 Fiduciary relationship

The bank and the customer also have a fiduciary relationship which means that the **bank is expected to act with the utmost good faith** in its relationship with the customer.

1.12 The duties of the bank

The bank has the following duties to its customers:

- It must honour customer's cheques as long as they are correctly made out, there is no legal reason for not honouring it and their customer has enough funds or overdraft limit to cover the amount of the cheque.

- The bank must credit cash/cheques paid in to the customer's account.

- If the customer makes a written request for repayment of funds in its account, for example by writing a cheque, the bank must repay the amounts on demand.

- The bank must comply with the customer's instructions by a direct debit mandate or standing order.

- The bank must provide a statement showing the transactions on the account and be prepared to provide details of the balance on the customer's account.

- The bank must respect the confidentiality of the customer's affairs unless the bank is required by law or public duty to disclose, or the interest of the bank requires disclosure or where the customer gives his consent for disclosure.

- The bank must tell the customer if there has been an attempt to forge the customer's signature on a cheque.

- The bank should use care and skill in its actions.

- The bank must provide reasonable notice if it is to close a customer's account.

1.13   Customer's duties

The customer has two main duties:

- to exercise care in drawing cheques such that fraud is not facilitated

- to tell the bank of any forgeries known of.

1.14   The rights of the bank

The rights of the bank are:

- to charge reasonable charges and commissions over and above interest

- to use the customer's money in any way provided that it is legal and morally acceptable

- to be repaid overdrawn balances on demand

- to be indemnified against possible losses when acting on a customer's behalf.

1.15   Services offered by merchant banks

Merchant banks may be subsidiaries of clearing banks, part of a large financial group of companies, or independent. Their main functions include:

- **Provision of financial advice** – mainly to larger commercial companies, on such aspects as the raising of finance, the investment of cash surpluses, and merger and acquisition activities. Such assistance can contribute significantly to a firm's financial management strategy.

- **Provision of finance** – merchant banks specialise in the provision of large, longer term lending through the money markets. They also have specialised 'issuing houses' that handle share and other security issues.

1.16   Institutional investors

Only about 20–25% of quoted company shares in the UK are currently held by private individuals.

The vast majority of equity finance for quoted companies comes from institutional investors, in particular the pension funds. The most important types of institutional investors are:

Pension fund – buys securities with the pension contributions it receives. These produce income to pay current pensioners, and provide for the need to pay future pensioners.

Insurance company – buys securities with the insurance premiums it receives. These produce income to pay for claims (for example, when life assurance policies mature) and provide for future claims. Investment trust – buys securities with the money raised by selling shares in the trust. The income and capital gains produced are distributed amongst the shareholders in the trust.

Unit trust – buys securities with the money raised by selling units in the trust. These produce income and capital gains to give the unit holders a return on their investment.

1.17   Venture capitalists

Venture capital is a **source of long-term (mainly equity) finance** where the investor relies on growth rather than income and is prepared to accept much greater risk.

It is normally provided under the condition of 'hands-on', the venture capitalist having a continuing involvement in the business of the company.

It is not subject to repayment on demand at a specified time, and realisation occurs only on the sale of the company or on flotation.

Venture capital is therefore a potentially valuable source of capital for small companies which would not prove attractive to the average investor on the Stock Exchange.

2 The Bank of England

2.1 Introduction

The Bank of England is the UK's central or national bank charged with overall control of the banking system in the interest of the nation.

The Bank of England is in the control of the UK government. The Governor, Deputy Governor and 16 directors are appointed by the Sovereign on the recommendation of the Prime Minister. Consequently, the Treasury is able to implement government policies through:

(a)   the use of monetary policy

(b)   the Bank's overall control of the banking system, and

(c)   the Bank's influence over the financial institutions.

The Bank of England acts as the government's bank in the widest possible sense, i.e. examining and anticipating banking problems.

2.2 The Bank of England's role as a banker

The Bank acts as banker:

(a)   to the government

(b)   to foreign central banks and international organisations.

All commercial banks have a bank account with the Bank which is used to settle debts between each other and to pay amounts due to the government.

2.3 The Bank of England's operations in the markets

- The Bank ensures implementation of government policy to control the economy by controlling the money market for short-term loans by the issue of Treasury bills.

- The Bank issues long-term government debt, referred to as gilt-edged securities or gilts.

- The Bank sets interest rates via a committee appointed by the government.

- The Bank manages the exchange rate to protect the pound. If sterling's value is too high the Bank sells sterling for foreign currencies, if its value is too low the Bank will buy sterling with its foreign currency reserves.

- The Bank meets the government's long-term borrowing requirements by open market operations on the Stock Exchange. The Bank is a lender of last resort and will provide funds for banks which are short of cash.

3 The money markets

3.1 Introduction

The term money markets covers a vast array of markets **buying and selling different forms of money or marketable securities**, which are short-term highly liquid investments that are readily convertible into cash. The money markets provide the financial institutions with a means of borrowing and investing to deal with short-term fluctuations.

The main traders in the money markets are banks, the government through the Bank of England, local authorities, brokers, jobbers and other intermediaries in the market.

3.2 Money market financial instruments

The main types of financial instrument that are traded in the money markets are:

- **Bills** – short-term financial assets that can be converted into cash by selling them in the discount market.

- **Deposits** – money in the bank accounts of banks and other financial intermediaries.

- **Commercial paper** – IOUs issued by large companies which can be either held to maturity or sold to third parties.

- **Certificates of deposit** (CDs) – a certificate for deposits of £50,000 or more for a fixed term which can be sold earlier than maturity in the CD market.

3.3 The primary market

This market consists of the **banks and securities firms and the Bank of England**. The primary market is used by the Bank to smooth out fluctuations in cash balances by buying bills and other short-term financial instruments from the financial institutions in order to provide more cash, and selling government bills to deal with any surplus cash.

3.4 The local authority market

In this market the local authorities borrow short-term funds by issuing local authority bills with a maturity of about one year.

3.5 The inter-bank market

This is a market for very short-term borrowing, often overnight, between the banks. It is used to smooth fluctuations in the banks' receipts and payments.

3.6 The foreign exchange market

Like the money market, the foreign exchange market operates through the general offices of its constituent banks. The aim of the foreign exchange dealers is to **secure supplies of foreign currency** as required to finance international trade.

The price of foreign currency is determined by demand and supply i.e. the demand for the country's goods and services by foreigners, and the supply of overseas goods and services which its own home nationals wish to buy.

3.7 The capital market

Many institutions apart from banks are used to provide capital, such as:

(a) **Issuing houses** who issue new shares or debentures for expanding firms.

(b) **Building societies** who collect funds for those wishing to purchase their own home.

(c) **Finance houses** who deal in the more risky but more profitable hire purchase field for financing purchase of consumer goods (e.g. cars).

(d) **Investment trusts and unit trusts** which accumulate small amounts from many individuals and purchase a balanced portfolio of investments, thus providing a good source of fixed capital for industry.

(e) **Insurance companies** who have large sums to invest from premiums received from insuring the public.

(f) The **Stock Exchange** which raises long-term capital not only via the provision of a market for existing stocks and shares but also by issuing new shares.

3.8 The Stock Exchange

Stock exchanges are based in many of the world's financial centres – such as New York, Tokyo and Paris. The function of such exchanges is to provide a **market place for the buying and selling of stocks and shares** so that companies can raise long-term finance and investors can buy or sell shares.

The Stock Exchange also provides a market for **government bonds or gilts.**

4 Government monetary policies

4.1 Introduction

Government monetary policies are the policies that are implemented by the Treasury and the Bank of England in order to **deal with the supply of money, interest rates and the availability of credit.**

4.2 Market operations

The government can influence the amount of money in the economy by restricting or encouraging bank lending. By selling attractively priced gilts the government takes money from financial institutions and individuals who pay for these gilts out of their bank accounts thereby reducing the banks' asset bases and the amount that they can lend.

The government also controls bank lending and influences the interest rate by the selling or buying of Treasury bills. By selling Treasury bills the government is taking money out of the system and by buying Treasury bills it can put money back into the system and through supply and demand can influence interest rates.

4.3 Interest rate policy

The Bank of England controls the interest rate through its operations in the primary money market. If interest rates rise then this reduces the demand for borrowing which in turn will have the effect of reducing consumer demand as less credit is available and the credit that is available is too costly.

4.4 Government spending and borrowing

If the government spends more than it raises in taxes then this will increase the money supply. This is known as the Public Sector Borrowing Requirement (PSBR). The government will wish to control the PSBR and to keep it within certain limits so as not to increase the money supply too much. If, however, the government spends less than it raises this will reduce the money supply, this is known as the Public Sector Debt Repayment (PSDR).

5 Summary

In this chapter we have summarised the main operations of the banks, the money markets and the government. The primary or retail banks deal in the transmission of money as high street banks, whereas the secondary banks deal with the wholesale business. The Bank of England plays an important role in controlling the banking system and operating the government's monetary policy and regulation of interest rates. Interest rates are controlled by the Bank in the primary market and short-term finance is provided to banks, financial institutions and large commercial organisations through the secondary market which is made up of the local authority market, the inter-bank market, the CD market, the inter-company market and the commercial paper market. Finally, we considered government monetary policy which is concerned with the supply of money, interest rates and the amount of credit that is available.

WORKBOOK

QUESTIONS

Key techniques questions

1. Liquidity

 Activity 1

Which of the following is not part of the working capital cycle?

A   Debtors

B   Fixed assets

C   Creditors

D   Stock

 Activity 2

Which is the correct formula for the working capital cycle?

A   Debtor days – stock days – creditor days

B   Debtor days – stock days + creditor days

C   Debtor days + stock days – creditor days

D   Debtor days + stock days + creditor days

Activity 3

A business has an average stock holding period of 45 days, receives payment from its customers in 30 days and pays its creditors in 38 days. What is the cash operating cycle in days for the business?

A   23 days

B   53 days

C   37 days

D   113 days

 Activity 4

Fill in the blanks in the diagram below:

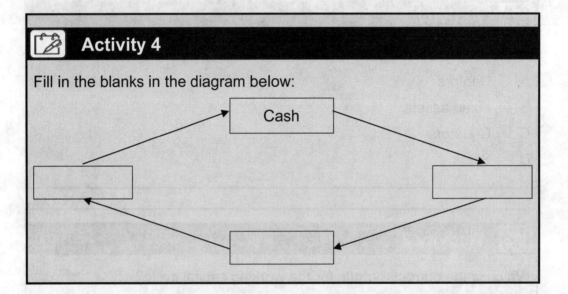

 Activity 5

Overtrading can occur when working capital levels are too low.

True or false?

Over-capitalisation can occur when working capital levels are too high.

True or false?

KAPLAN PUBLISHING

2 Cash budgets

Activity 6

Payments that relate to the purchase of fixed assets would be classified as:

A   Capital payments

B   Regular revenue receipts

C   Drawings

D   Exceptional receipts

Activity 7

Income received from an insurance claim for lost stock would be classified as:

A   Capital payments

B   Regular revenue receipts

C   Drawings

D   Exceptional receipts

Activity 8

The profit and loss account for C Lad's business for the quarter ended June is as follows:

	£	£
Sales		30,582
Less: Purchases		(12,210)
Gross profit		18,372
Less: Expenses		
Wages	1,000	
Rent of office	500	
Insurance of machinery	750	
Electricity	350	
Depreciation	210	
		(2,810)
Profit		15,562

Extracts from the balance sheet at 1 April and 30 June show the following:

	1 April	30 June
	£	£
Debtors	8,700	5,200
Creditors	420	375
Accruals – Electricity	250	300
Prepayments – Rent of office	400	350

Calculate the actual business cash receipts and cash payments for the quarter to 30 June

	Working	£
Sales receipts	30582 + 8760 – 5200	34082 ✓
Purchases	420 + 12210 – 357	12255 ✓
Wages		1000 ✓
Rent of office	– 400 + 350 + 500	450 ✓
Insurance of machinery		750 ✓
Electricity	350 + 250 – 300	300
Depreciation		0

Activity 9

The following data and estimates are available for ABC Ltd for June, July and August:

	June £	July £	August £
Sales	45,000	50,000	60,000
Wages	12,000	13,000	14,500
Overheads	8,500	9,500	9,000

The following information is available regarding direct materials:

	June £	July £	August £	September £
Opening stock	5,000	3,500	6,000	4,000
Material usage	8,000	9,000	10,000	
Closing stock	3,500	6,000	4,000	

Notes:

(1) 10% of sales are for cash, the balance is received the following month.

   The amount to be received in June for May's sales is £29,500.

(2) Wages are paid in the month they are incurred.

(3) Overheads include £1,500 per month for depreciation. Overheads are settled the month following. £6,500 is to be paid in June for May's overheads.

(4) Purchases of direct materials are paid for in the month purchased.

(5) The opening cash balance in June is £11,750.

(6) A tax bill of £25,000 is to be paid in July.

Task

(a)   Calculate the amount of direct material purchases in EACH of the
      months of June, July and August.

	June £	July £	August £
Material usage			
Closing stock			
	_____	_____	_____
Less: Opening stock			
	_____	_____	_____
Purchases			
	_____	_____	_____

(b)   Prepare cash budgets for June, July and August.

	June £	July £	August £
Receipts of cash			
Cash sales			
Credit sales			
	_____	_____	_____
	_____	_____	_____
Cash payments			
Wages			
Overheads			
Direct materials			
Taxation			
	_____	_____	_____
	_____	_____	_____
Surplus/(deficit) for month			
Opening balance			
	_____	_____	_____
Closing balance			
	_____	_____	_____

Activity 10

From the following statements, prepare a month-by-month cash budget for the six months to 31 December.

(a) **Revenue budget (i.e. trading and profit and loss account)**

Six months to 31 December (all revenue/costs accrue evenly over the six months)

	£	£
Sales (cash received one month in arrears)		1,200
Cost of sales:		
Paid one month in arrear	900	
Paid in month of purchase	144	
Depreciation	72	
	——	1,116
		——
Budgeted profit		84
		——

(b) **Capital budget**

	£000	£000
Payments for new plant:		
July	12	
August	25	
September	13	
November	50	
	——	100
Increase in stocks, payable August		20
		——
		120
		——
Receipts:		
New issue of share capital (October)		30
		——

(c) **Balance sheet**

	Actual 1 July
	£000
Assets side:	
Fixed assets	720
Stocks	100
Debtors	210
Cash	40
	1,070
Liabilities side:	
Capital and reserves	856
Taxation (payable December)	30
Creditors – trade	160
Dividends (payable August)	24
	1,070

	Jul £000	Aug £000	Sep £000	Oct £000	Nov £000	Dec £000	Total £000
Receipts:							
Sales							
New issue of share capital							
Payments:							
Expenses and purchases							
Expenses and purchases							
Plant							
Stock							
Tax							
Dividends							
Surplus/(deficiency)							
Opening balance							
Closing balance							

Activity 11

XYZ Ltd has the following forecast sales at list price for the nine months to 29 February 20X2:

June	£40,000	September	£48,000	December	£44,000
July	£44,000	October	£40,000	January	£42,000
August	£50,000	November	£45,000	February	£50,000

60% of the company's sales are on credit, payable in the month after sale. Cash sales attract a 5% discount off list price.

Purchases amount to 40% of selling price, and these are paid for two months after delivery.

Wages comprise a fixed sum of £2,000 per month plus a variable element equal to 10% of sales; these are payable in the month they are incurred.

Fixed costs amount to £7,500 per month, payable one month in arrears, of which £1,500 is depreciation.

XYZ Ltd has capital expenditure/receipts scheduled as follows:

Acquisitions:	£
September	15,000
November	10,000
February	4,000
Disposal:	
October	8,000

Corporation tax, payable in November, amounts to £44,000.

The bank balance on 1 September 20X1 is expected to be £5,000.

Task

Prepare a cash flow forecast for XYZ Ltd for EACH of the six months from September 20X1 to February 20X2, using a row and column format.

	Sept £	Oct £	Nov £	Dec £	Jan £	Feb £
Receipts:						
Cash sales						
Credit sales						
Capital						
Payments:						
Purchases						
Wages						
Fixed costs						
Capital						
Corporation tax						
Surplus/(Deficit)						
Balance b/f						
Balance c/f						

Activity 12

Refer to the budget data sheet in the data that follows. The date is 1December 20X7. You are required to use this information to produce a cash forecast for Blether Telecom for the period to 31 March 20X8. The cash forecast should clearly show the opening and closing cash position for each month, as well as the net cash flow for the period. It might help you to complete the table of estimated call volumes before calculating revenues and costs.

BLETHER TELECOM

BUDGET DATA SHEET

Revenue:

National call (peak)	£0.048 per minute
National call (off peak)	£0.021 per minute
International call (peak)	£0.105 per minute (average rate)
International call (off peak)	£0.078 per minute (average rate)

Call volume (previous three months):

Type of call	Sep 20X7 (minutes)	Oct 20X7 (minutes)	Nov 20X7 (minutes)
National call (peak)	1,195,687	1,203,360	1,231,049
National call (off-peak)	30,651	30,914	31,982
International call (peak)	295,999	296,771	319,754
International call (off-peak)	14,478	14,637	15,980
Total	1,536,815	1,545,682	1,598,765

Projected call mix in the period to March 20X8 (based on average over previous 12 months):

Type of call	Percentage share of call volume
National call (peak)	78%
National call (off-peak)	2%
International call (peak)	19%
International call (off-peak)	1%
Total	100%

Note: assume call mix will be as above to March 20X8.

Projected growth rates (straight-line) in call volumes over the next four months:

Month	Dec	Jan	Feb	Mar
Cumulative Growth rate (%)	2	5	9	11

(i.e. all based on November volume). Assume the mix of call volumes is unchanged.

Direct costs:

Type of call	Cost to Blether Telecom per minute
National call (peak)	0.031
National call (off-peak)	0.014
International call (peak)	0.067
International call (off-peak)	0.050

Overheads

*   Staff costs, £13,350 per month, with a rise of 3.5 per cent in March. Marketing costs, £5,000 per month. In addition a targeted advertising campaign will be undertaken in the next six months, with costs of £22,000 paid in March.

*   Other overheads of £9,000 per month are incurred. This includes depreciation of £3,000 per month and a provision for doubtful debts of £200 per month.

*   Premises costs are paid for by direct debit each month and average £9,350 per month.

Other payments

*   A tax bill of £8,500 is payable in December.

*   Dividend payment of £8,000 is to be paid in March.

*   Interest is payable on a loan of £275,000 at a rate of 9% per annum, with one year's interest paid in February.

Working capital management

*   Customers are billed monthly, with payment being made (on average) 60 days in arrears.

*   Blether Telecom pays the operating companies supplying the communications monthly, 30 days in arrears.

*   The cash balance at bank on 31 October 20X7 was £51,784.

	Actual Nov	Forecast Dec	Forecast Jan	Forecast Feb	Forecast Mar
Revenue					
National (peak)					
National (off-peak)					
International (peak)					
International (off-peak)					
Subtotal					
Direct cost					
National (peak)					
National (off-peak)					
International (peak)					
International (off-peak)					
Subtotal					
Overheads					
Marketing					
Staff costs					
Other overheads					
Premises					
Taxation					
Dividends					
Interest					
Subtotal					
Net cash flow					
Opening cash flow					
Closing cash flow					

Note – Call volumes (mins)

	Actual Nov	Forecast Dec	Forecast Jan	Forecast Feb	Forecast Mar
TOTAL CALLS					
National (peak)					
National (off-peak)					
International (peak)					
International (off-peak)					

Activity 13

Refer to the memo from John Powell, the memo from Mark Bennett and the memo from Victoria Bartlett. You are required to:

- prepare a cash flow forecast for the first three months of next year for the new division;

FASTINFO LTD
MEMO

To: Henry Naem

From: John Powell

Date: 14 January

Subject: Work for this week

Henry

I have been unexpectedly called up to Scotland for the week to look at a possible new supplier. As you know there is a lot of urgent work on and I need you to prepare the following for me.

There is a strategy meeting with the Managing Director next week and I need to have some cash flow information about the possible new division. I have left cash flow predictions for the first three months of next year from Mark and Victoria on my desk. I am particularly interested in finding out the impact on the bank balance if debtors were given an extra month's credit.

FASTINFO LTD
MEMO

To: John Powell

From: Mark Bennett

Date: 12 January

Subject: New Division

Further to our conversation I have put together the forecast cash expenditure for the new division next year:

- new equipment will cost a total of £200,000. We need to buy it in January and put down a deposit of £50,000 on 1 January. I have negotiated instalments for the remainder; three equal instalments payable on 1 February, 1 May and 1 September next year. We can get a grant for part of the cost (10%) and this will be received on 1 January also;

- rent for premises will amount to £5,000 per quarter payable in advance, with the first payment being 1 January;

- wages will be £6,000 per month, payable on the last day of the month worked;

- purchases will amount to £10,000 in each of the first two months, then £12,000 in the next two months, increasing by £2,000 every two months for the rest of the year. Purchases will be paid for two months after they have been received.

I look forward to seeing the cash flow forecast and discussing it further.

With regards.

Mark

FASTINFO LTD
MEMO

To: John Powell

From: Victoria Bartlett

Date: 13 January

Subject: Future sales from new division

I have put together some forecast sales for the first three months of next year for the new division. I have been quite conservative so these figures should be achieved with relative ease.

	January £	February £	March £
Cash sales	12,000	12,500	13,000
Credit sales	12,000	12,500	13,000
Total	24,000	25,000	26,000

Credit sales will be payable by the end of the month after the sale was made. Selling and administration costs will amount to 10% of the sales made in the month and they are payable in cash as incurred.

With regards.

Victoria

CASH FLOW FORMAT

CASH FLOW FORECAST FOR THE FIRST THREE MONTHS OF NEXT YEAR, NEW DIVISION

	January £	February £	March £
CASH RECEIVED Sales: cash credit			
Grant			
Total			
CASH PAID Equipment: deposit			
Equipment: instalment			
Rent			
Wages			
Purchases			
Selling/administration			
Total			
Net cash flow			
B/F cash balance			
C/F cash balance			

3 Forecasting and monitoring cash flows

 Activity 14

The managers of a company are preparing revenue plans for the first quarter of next year. The figures below refer to the revenue for the year just past. Compete the table to calculate the monthly sales volume trend, he monthly variations from the trend and then the prediction for the January to March for next year.

Jan	Feb	Mar	Apr	May	Jun	Jul	Aug	Sept	Oct	Nov	Dec
49	37	58	50	38	59	51	40	60	52	42	61

Month	Sales volume	3 Month Trend	Monthly variation
Jan	49		
Feb	37		
Mar	58		
Apr	50		
May	38		
Jun	60		
Jul	51		
Aug	40		
Sept	61		
Oct	53		
Nov	43		
Dec	61		

Month	Forecast sales trend	Variation	Forecast sale volume
Jan			
Feb			
Mar			

Activity 15

Below is the sales data for January to December 20Y1 and January to March 20Y2. Calculate the 5 month trend and monthly variation

Month	Sales volume	5 Month Trend	Monthly variation
Jan	150		
Feb	310		
Mar	400		
Apr	490		
May	750		
Jun	180		
Jul	340		
Aug	430		
Sept	520		
Oct	780		
Nov	210		
Dec	370		
Jan	460		
Feb	550		
Mar	810		

What will be the predicted sales volume for December 20Y2

A   610

B   476

C   526

D   482

Activity 16

The company uses an industry sector index to calculate the selling price of its product. The price to due to be revised in March in line with the index. The current selling price of £45 was set when the index was 132. The forecast index is as follows:

January	145
February	152
March	154
April	157

What will be the selling price to the nearest pence in March?

A   £37.83

B   £51.82

C   £38.57

D   £52.50

 Activity 17

FASTINFO LTD
MEMO

To: Henry Naem

From: John Powell

Date: 14 January

Subject: Work for this week

Henry

I have left a copy of the cash flow forecast and actual cash flow for the final three months of last year on my desk. Please compare the two and write me a memo listing any major differences and suggested corrective action.

CASH FLOW FORECAST FOR THE LAST THREE MONTHS OF LAST YEAR, WHOLE COMPANY

	October £000	November £000	December £000
CASH RECEIVED			
Cash sales	1,300	1,400	1,420
Credit sales	1,200	1,200	1,300
Sale of assets	2	11	5
TOTAL	2,502	2,611	2,725
CASH PAID			
land	1,000	–	–
machinery	200	75	75
vehicles	300	200	200
Rent	250	250	250
Wages	30	31	32
Purchases	1,500	1,600	1,800
Selling/administration	25	27	28
Net cash flow	–803	428	340
B/F cash balance	20	–783	–355
C/F cash balance	–783	–355	–15

ACTUAL CASH FLOW FOR THE LAST THREE MONTHS OF LAST YEAR, WHOLE COMPANY

	October £000	November £000	December £000
CASH RECEIVED			
Cash sales	1,200	1,100	1,100
Credit sales	1,100	1,150	1,200
Sale of machine	1	20	10
TOTAL	2,301	2,270	2,310
CASH PAID			
land	1,000	–	–
machinery	300	75	75
vehicles	320	210	240
Rent	250	250	250
Wages	38	35	37
Purchases	1,600	1,600	1,800
Selling/administration	28	29	29
Net cash flow	–1,235	71	–121
B/F cash balance	20	–1,215	–1,144
C/F cash balance	–1,215	–1,144	–1,265

RECONCILIATION OF ACTUAL TO BUDGET

	Actual £	Budget £	£
Budgeted closing bank balance			
Cash sales:			
Credit sales:			
Sale of assets			
Purchase of land			
Purchase of machinery			
Purchase of vehicles			
Rent			
Wages			
Purchases			
Selling/administration			
Actual closing bank balance			

Activity 18

FASTINFO LTD
MEMO

To: Henry Naem

From: John Powell

Date: 14 January

Subject: Work for this week

Henry

I have left a copy of the cash flow forecast for the next three months for a new venture. Please can you calculate the effect on the balance if the debtors were given an extra months grace.

CASH FLOW FORECAST FOR THE FIRST THREE MONTHS OF NEXT YEAR, NEW DIVISION

	January £	February £	March £
CASH RECEIVED			
Sales: cash	12,000	12,500	13,000
Sales: credit	–	12,000	12,500
Grant	20,000		
Total	32,000	24,500	25,500
CASH PAID			
Equipment: deposit	50,000		
Equipment: instalment		50,000	
Rent	5,000		
Wages	6,000	6,000	6,000
Purchases			10,000
Selling/administration	2,400	2,500	2,600
Total	63,400	58,500	18,600
Net cash flow	–31,400	–34,000	6,900
B/F cash balance	0	–31,400	–65,400
C/F cash balance	–31,400	–65,400	–58,500

IMPACT ON BANK BALANCE IF DEBTORS PAY ONE MONTH LATER

	January £	February £	March £
CASH RECEIVED			
Sales: cash			
Sales: credit			
Grant			
	___	___	___
Total			
	___	___	___
CASH PAID			
	___	___	___
Net cash flow			
B/F cash balance			
C/F cash balance			

Activity 19

Variances between budget and actual cash flows can occur for number of reasons. Match the variance below with the possible course of action.

Variance		Action
Receipts from debtors is less than budget		Negotiate a settlement discount
Payments to suppliers are being made earlier than planned		Change supplier
A new machine was bought that was not in the budget		Improve credit control
Prices of raw materials have increased		Reduce overtime working
Labour costs have increased		Improve communication

4 Raising finance

 Activity 20

You have performed a cash flow budget for the coming year and have noticed that there is going to be a cash deficit caused by the need to by new machinery for the production line. What would be the better source of finance for this deficit?

Overdraft or loan?

Activity 21

You have performed a cash flow budget for the coming year and have noticed that there is going to be a cash deficit caused by creditors changing their payment terms. There will be a short term demand for extra cash flow. What would be the better source of finance for this deficit?

Overdraft or loan?

 Activity 22

Which of the following best describes the main features of an overdraft?

A   Interest rates are low; it is repayable on demand; it is useful for capital purchases

B   Interest rates are high; it is repayable on demand; it is useful for capital purchases

C   Interest rates are low; it is repayable on demand; it is a short term form of finance

D   Interest rates are high; it is repayable on demand; it is a short term form of finance

 Activity 23

Which of the following best describes the main features of a bank loan?

A   Interest rates are low; repayments can be negotiated; it is useful for capital purchases

B   Interest rates are high; repayments can be negotiated; it is useful for capital purchases

C   Interest rates are low; repayments can be negotiated; it is a short term form of finance

D   Interest rates are high; repayments can be negotiated; it is a short term form of finance

Activity 24

Finalite is planning to expand their production facilities. The expansion plans require new machinery at a cost of £55,000 and a working capital injection of £20,000.

There are 3 different options for funding the expansion:

Option 1

- A bank loan of £55,000 secured on the new machinery. Capital repayments are to be made of equal amounts over 5 years. The interest rate is fixed at 5% per annum calculated on the capital balance outstanding at the beginning of each year.

- An arrangement equal to 0.7% of the bank loan is payable at the beginning of the loan term.

- The bank is also offering an overdraft facility of £22,000 which attracts an annual interest rate of 11%. Finalite believes that they will have an average overdraft of £11,000 for the first 6 months of the first year.

Option 2

- A bank loan of £75,000 secured on the assets of the partnership. Capital repayments are to be made over 5 years, with a 5 month payment holiday at the beginning of the loan term.

- The interest rate is fixed at 7% per annum for the first 2 years and will then revert to a variable interest rate 2% above the base rate.

- An arrangement fee equal to 0.8% of the bank loan is payable at the beginning of the loan term.

- No overdraft facility will be required.

Option 3

- Finalites' two owners each take out a personal secured loan for £37,500 repayable over 3 years at an interest rate of 5%. These monies will then be loaned to the partnership as increased capital. Interest of 8% per annum is payable by the business to the two owners.

- No overdraft facility will be required.

Required

Calculate the cost of each of the above options for the first year. Which of the 3 methods would you recommend?

	Loan Interest £	Arrangement fee £	Overdraft interest £	Total cost £
Option 1				
Option 2				
Option 3				

Recommendation:

5 Investing surplus funds

 Activity 25

Use the pick lists to complete the following sentences:

Certificates of deposit are certificates issued by [banks/local authorities/government]. They [can/cannot] be traded on a market. They are considered to be a [low risk/high risk] investment.

Local authority short term loans are certificates issued by [banks/local authorities/government]. They [can/cannot] be traded on a market. They are considered to be a [low risk/high risk] investment.

Government securities are also known as [gold-edged/gilt-edged/gilted] securities. They [can/cannot] be traded on a market. They are considered to be a [low risk/high risk] investment.

Activity 26

Four possible investment options are available:

Option 1

Investment of £50,000 required, there is a 60 day notice period, the investment includes some shares in the portfolio and the interest rate is 5% per annum.

Option 2

Investment should be between £60,000 and £30,000, there is a 30 day notice period, interest is 3%, there are no shares included in the investment portfolio.

Option 3

Investment portfolio consists of stocks and shares but has a projected interest rate of 8%. There is a minimum investment of £35,000 required and a 45 day notice period exists.

Option 4

A low risk investment opportunity with a guaranteed return of 2.5%, the minimum investment required is £40,000 and 10 working days notice must be given for withdrawals.

The treasury department has the following policy for investing surplus funds:

It must be possible to access the cash invested within 30 days

The maximum investment amount is £50,000

The interest rate must be 2.5% above base rate, which is currently 0.5%

The investment must be low risk

Complete the table below and decide which policy can be invested in, if any

	Convertible within 30 days?	Investment £50,000 or below?	Interest rate 2.5% above base rate?	Low risk?	Invest?
Option 1					
Option 2					
Option 3					
Option 4					

ANSWERS

Key techniques answers

1 Liquidity

Activity 1

Answer B

Fixed assets are not part of the working capital cycle – current assets are.

Activity 2

Answer C

Debtor days + stock days – creditor days

Activity 3

Answer C

45 + 30 – 38 = 37 days

Activity 4

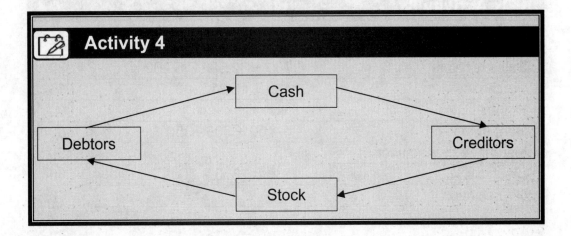

Activity 5

Overtrading can occur when working capital levels are too low.

True

Over-capitalisation can occur when working capital levels are too high.

True

2 Cash budgets

 Activity 6

Answer A

Fixed assets would require a large capital payment to be made

 Activity 7

Answer D

Income from an insurance claim would not be expected as part of day to day trading

 Activity 8

	Working	£
Sales receipts	8,700 + 30,582 – 5,200	34,082
Purchases	420 + 12,210 – 375	12,255
Wages		1,000
Rent of office	–400 + 500 +350	450
Insurance of machinery		750
Electricity	250 +350 – 300	30
Depreciation		0

Activity 9

(a)

	June £	July £	August £
Material usage	8,000	9,000	10,000
Closing stock	3,500	6,000	4,000
	11,500	15,000	14,000
Less: Opening stock	5,000	3,500	6,000
Purchases	6,500	11,500	8,000

(b)

Cash budgets, June – August

	June £	July £	August £
Receipts of cash			
Cash sales	4,500	5,000	6,000
Credit sales	29,500	40,500	45,000
	34,000	45,500	51,000
Cash payments			
Wages	12,000	13,000	14,500
Overheads	6,500	7,000	8,000
Direct materials	6,500	11,500	8,000
Taxation	–	25,000	–
	25,000	56,500	30,500
Surplus/(deficit) for month	9,000	(11,000)	20,500
Opening balance	11,750	20,750	9,750
Closing balance	20,750	9,750	30,250

Tutorial note: The main points to watch out for are sales receipts and overheads. Tackle sales receipts by calculating separate figures for cash sales (10% of total sales, received in the month of sale) and credit sales (90% of last month's sales). For overheads, remember that depreciation is not a cash expense and must therefore be stripped out of the overheads cash cost.

Activity 10

	Jul £000	Aug £000	Sep £000	Oct £000	Nov £000	Dec £000	Total £000
Receipts:							
Sales	210	200	200	200	200	200	1,210
New issue of share capital	–	–	–	30	–	–	30
Payments:							
Expenses and purchases	160	150	150	150	150	150	910
Expenses and purchases	24	24	24	24	24	24	144
Plant	12	25	13	–	50	–	100
Stock	–	20	–	–	–	–	20
Tax	–	–	–	–	–	30	30
Dividends	–	24	–	–	–	–	24
	196	243	187	174	224	204	1,228
Surplus/(deficiency)	14	(43)	13	56	(24)	(4)	12
Opening balance	40	54	11	24	80	56	40
Closing balance	54	11	24	80	56	52	52

Activity 11

	Sept £	Oct £	Nov £	Dec £	Jan £	Feb £
Receipts:						
Cash sales (W1)	18,240	15,200	17,100	16,720	15,960	19,000
Credit sales (W2)	30,000	28,800	24,000	27,000	26,400	25,200
Capital		8,000				
	48,240	52,000	41,100	43,720	42,360	44,200
Payments:						
Purchases	17,600	20,000	19,200	16,000	18,000	17,600
Wages (W3)	6,800	6,000	6,500	6,400	6,200	7,000
Fixed costs (W4)	6,000	6,000	6,000	6,000	6,000	6,000
Capital	15,000		10,000			4,000
Corporation tax			44,000			
	45,400	32,000	85,700	28,400	30,200	34,600
Surplus/(Deficit)	2,840	20,000	(44,600)	15,320	12,160	9,600
Balance b/f	5,000	7,840	27,840	(16,760)	(1,440)	10,720
Balance c/f	7,840	27,840	(16,760)	(1,440)	10,720	20,320

Workings

(W1) Since 60% of sales are credit sales, 40% are cash sales, e.g.

	£
September cash sales = £48,000 × 40% =	19,200
5% discount on £19,200	960
	18,240

(W2) August credit sales are paid in September, and so on.

Credit sales = 60% so the September receipt = 60% × £50,000 = £30,000.

(W3) 10% of sales + £2,000

e.g. September: (10% × £48,000) + £2,000 = £6,800

(W4) Fixed costs: £6,000 (£7,500 − £1,500)

Activity 12

	Nov	Dec	Jan	Feb	Mar
Revenue					
National (peak)	57,393	57,761	59,090	61,055	62,851
National (off-peak)	644	649	672	685	705
International (peak)	31,080	31,161	33,574	32,533	33,490
International (off-peak)	1,129	1,142	1,246	1,272	1,309
Sub total	90,246	90,713	94,582	95,545	98,355
Direct costs					
National (peak)	37,304	38,163	39,431	40,591	42,137
National (off-peak)	433	448	457	470	488
International (peak)	19,884	21,424	20,759	21,370	22,184
International (off-peak)	732	799	815	839	871
Sub total	58,353	60,834	61,462	63,270	65,680
Overheads					
Marketing	5,000	5,000	5,000	5,000	27,000
Staff costs	13,350	13,350	13,350	13,350	13,817
Other overheads	5,800	5,800	5,800	5,800	5,800
Premises	9,350	9,350	9,350	9,350	9,350
Taxation		8,500			
Dividends					8,000
Interest				24,750	
Sub total	33,500	42,000	33,500	58,250	63,967
Net cash flow	−1,607	−12,121	−380	−25,975	−31,292
Opening cash flow	51,784	50,177	38,056	37,676	11,701
Closing cash flow	50,177	38,056	37,676	11,701	19,591

Note: Call volumes (mins)

	Nov	Dec	Jan	Feb	Mar
Total calls	1,598,765	1,630,740	1,678,703	1,742,654	1,774,629
National (peak)	1,231,049	1,271,977	1,309,388	1,359,270	1,384,211
National (off-peak)	31,982	32,615	33,574	34,853	35,493
International (peak)	319,754	309,841	318,954	331,104	337,179
International (off-peak)	15,980	16,307	16,787	17,427	17,746

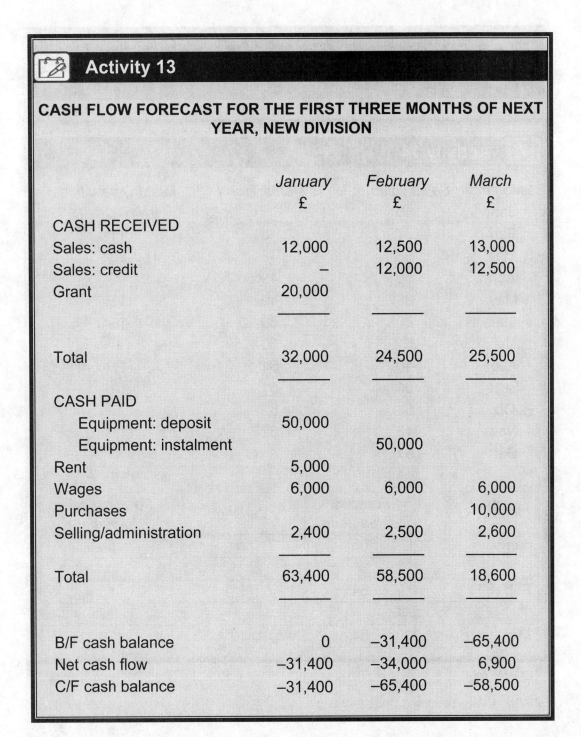

Activity 13

CASH FLOW FORECAST FOR THE FIRST THREE MONTHS OF NEXT YEAR, NEW DIVISION

	January £	February £	March £
CASH RECEIVED			
Sales: cash	12,000	12,500	13,000
Sales: credit	–	12,000	12,500
Grant	20,000		
Total	32,000	24,500	25,500
CASH PAID			
Equipment: deposit	50,000		
Equipment: instalment		50,000	
Rent	5,000		
Wages	6,000	6,000	6,000
Purchases			10,000
Selling/administration	2,400	2,500	2,600
Total	63,400	58,500	18,600
B/F cash balance	0	–31,400	–65,400
Net cash flow	–31,400	–34,000	6,900
C/F cash balance	–31,400	–65,400	–58,500

3 Forecasting and monitoring cash flows

Activity 14

Month	Sales volume	3 Month Trend	Monthly variation
Jan	49		
Feb	37	48	(11)
Mar	58	48	10
Apr	50	49	1
May	38	49	(11)
Jun	60	50	10
Jul	51	50	1
Aug	40	51	(11)
Sept	61	51	10
Oct	53	52	1
Nov	43	52	(11)
Dec	61		

Month	Forecast sales trend	Variation	Forecast sale volume
Jan	53	1	54
Feb	54	(11)	43
Mar	54	10	64

Activity 15

Month	Sales volume	5 Month Trend	Monthly variation
Jan	150		
Feb	310		
Mar	400	420	(20)
Apr	490	426	64
May	750	432	318
Jun	180	438	(258)
Jul	340	444	(104)
Aug	430	450	(20)
Sept	520	456	64
Oct	780	462	318
Nov	210	468	(258)
Dec	370	474	(104)
Jan	460	480	(20)
Feb	550		
Mar	810		

What will be the predicted sales volume for December 20Y2

A   610

480 + (6×11) +64 = 610

Activity 16

Answer D

45/132 × 154 = £52.50

Activity 17

RECONCILIATION OF ACTUAL TO BUDGET

	Actual	Budget	£
Budgeted closing bank balance			(15,000)
Cash sales:	3,400,000	4,120,000	(720,000)
Credit sales:	3,450,000	3,700,000	(250,000)
Sale of assets	31,000	18,000	13,000
Purchase of land	1,000,000	1,000,000	0
Purchase of machinery	450,000	350,000	(100,000)
Purchase of vehicles	770,000	700,000	(70,000)
Rent	750,000	750,000	0
Wages	110,000	93,000	(17,000)
Purchases	5,000,000	4,900,000	(100,000)
Selling/administration	86,000	80,000	(6,000)
Actual closing bank balance			(1,265,000)

KAPLAN PUBLISHING

Activity 18

IMPACT ON BANK BALANCE IF DEBTORS PAY ONE MONTH LATER

Amended cash received

	January £	February £	March £
CASH RECEIVED			
Sales: cash	12,000	12,500	13,000
Sales: credit	–	–	12,000
Grant	20,000		
Total	32,000	12,500	25,000
CASH PAID	63,400	58,500	18,600
Net cash flow	–31,400	–46,000	6,400
B/F cash balance	0	–31,400	–77,400
C/F cash balance	–31,400	–77,400	–71,000

Activity 19

Variance	Action
Receipts from debtors is less than budget	Improve credit control
Payments to suppliers are being made earlier than planned	Negotiate a settlement discount
A new machine was bought that was not in the budget	Improve communication
Prices of raw materials have increased	Change supplier
Labour costs have increased	Reduce overtime working

4 Raising finance

Activity 20

Loan

Activity 21

Overdraft

Activity 22

Answer D

Activity 23

Answer A

Activity 24

	Loan Interest £	Arrangement fee £	Overdraft interest £	Total cost £
Option 1	2,750	385	605	3,740
Option 2	5,250	600	0	5,850
Option 3	6,000	0	0	6,000

Recommendation: Option 1

Workings

Option 1

Loan interest 55,000 × 5% = £2,750

Arrangement fee 55,000 × 0.7% = £385

Overdraft interest 11,000 × 11% ×6/12 = £605

Option 2

Loan Interest 75,000 × 7% = £5,250

Arrangement fee 75,000 × 0.8% = £600

Option 3

Loan interest (37,500 × 8%) × 2 = £6,000

5 Investing surplus funds

 Activity 25

Certificates of deposit are certificates issued by banks. They can be traded on a market. They are considered to be a low risk investment.

Local authority short term loans are certificates issued by local authorities. They can be traded on a market. They are considered to be a low risk investment.

Government securities are also known as gilt-edged securities. They can be traded on a market. They are considered to be a low risk investment.

Activity 26

	Convertible within 30 days?	Investment £50,000 or below?	Interest rate 2.5% above base rate?	Low risk?	Invest?
Option 1	N	Y	Y	N	N
Option 2	Y	Y	Y	Y	Y
Option 3	N	Y	Y	N	N
Option 4	Y	Y	N	Y	N

INDEX

KAPLAN PUBLISHING